TABLE OF CONTENTS

Introduction v

Unit 1: Guide to Critical Thinking

Purpose of This Unit 1
When is an Argument Not a Fight? 1
Assertions 2
Evidence 2
Reasoning 4
- by Cause and Effect 5
- by Comparison 7
- by Generalization 8
- by Proof 11
- by Debate 13

Assumptions 15
Values 16
Arguments—Model and Five Main Parts 18

Unit 2: New Republic

Lesson 1 Identifying Sources 19
Lesson 2 Evaluating Sources 20
Lesson 3 Determining Causes and Effects 22
Lesson 4 Evaluating Cause-and-Effect Reasoning 24
Lesson 5 Identifying and Evaluating Comparisons 27
Lesson 6 How Did Early Industrialization Change Small New England Villages? 29
Lesson 7 What Were the Characteristics of the Ideal Woman in the Early 1800s? 40
Lesson 8 What Arguments Were Made for and against Women's Rights? 48
Lesson 9 Was Andrew Jackson a Representative of the Common People? 71

Unit 3: Slavery

Lesson 10 Identifying and Evaluating Evidence 77
Lesson 11 Assessing Cause and Effect 80
Lesson 12 Analyzing Generalizations 82
Lesson 13 Identifying and Assessing Types of Reasoning 84
Lesson 14 Was Slavery Good or Bad? 86
Lesson 15 How Did Slavery Affect Slaves? 91
Lesson 16 What Was It Like to Be a Slave? 100
Lesson 17 What Do Visual Sources Show about Slavery? 128
Lesson 18 Were Slaves Fed an Adequate Diet? 137

Unit 4: Civil War

Lesson 19 Assessing the Reliability of Sources 147
Lesson 20 Analyzing Cause-and-Effect 149
Lesson 21 Identifying and Evaluating Types of Reasoning 152
Lesson 22 Identifying and Evaluating Proof and Debating Reasoning 155
Lesson 23 Which Side Caused the Firing on Fort Sumter? 158
Lesson 24 What Do Historians Assume about the Causes of War? 160
Lesson 25 What Were the Causes of the Civil War? 167
Lesson 26 What Led to the Emancipation Proclamation and England's Neutrality in the Civil War? 177
Lesson 27 What Role Did Racism Play in the Civil War and Nineteenth-Century America? 183

Bibliography: Major Sources Used for Lessons 189

CRITICAL THINKING IN UNITED STATES HISTORY SERIES

BOOK TWO

NEW REPUBLIC TO CIVIL WAR

KEVIN O'REILLY

SERIES TITLES:
BOOK 1–COLONIES TO CONSTITUTION
BOOK 2–NEW REPUBLIC TO CIVIL WAR
BOOK 3–RECONSTRUCTION TO PROGRESSIVISM
BOOK 4–SPANISH-AMERICAN WAR TO VIETNAM WAR

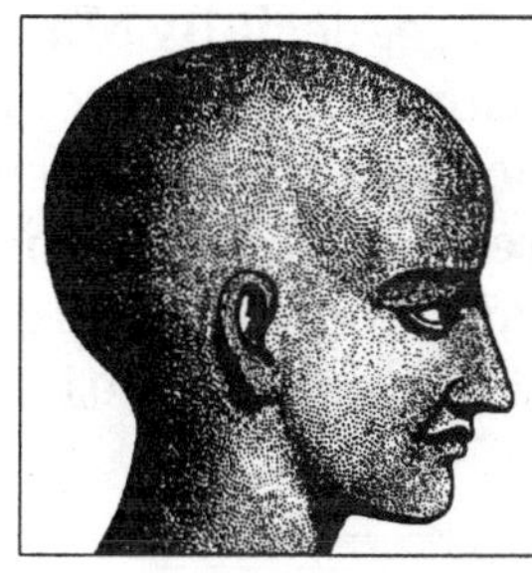

CRITICAL THINKING BOOKS & SOFTWARE
P.O. Box 448 • Pacific Grove • CA 93950-0448
Phone 800-458-4849 • FAX 408-393-3277
ISBN 0-89455-415-8
Printed in the United States of America

ABOUT THE AUTHOR

Kevin O'Reilly is a social studies teacher at Hamilton-Wenham Regional High School in Massachusetts. He was named by *Time* magazine and the National Council for the Social Studies as the 1986 Outstanding Social Studies Teacher in the United States. In addition to these four volumes on Critical Thinking in United States History, Mr. O'Reilly is the coauthor of *Critical Viewing: Stimulant to Critical Thinking* (also published by Critical Thinking Press & Software, formerly Midwest Publications) and the author of "Escalation," a computer simulation on the Vietnam War (Kevin O'Reilly, 6 Mason Street, Beverly, MA 01915). Mr. O'Reilly, who has a Master of Arts Degree in History, is an editor of the *New England Journal of History*. He conducts workshops throughout the United States on critical thinking, critical viewing, and decision-making.

FOR

Lynn
with all my love

ACKNOWLEDGMENTS

I would like to thank the following for their help: the Schlesinger Library staff for its help in researching women's history both in a summer institute and for Lesson 7 of this book; Old Sturbridge Village for permission to use "A Farm Woman's Diary" and "Accounts: The Davis Family" and the Baker Library at Harvard University as well for the Davis Family (Lesson 6); the Library of Congress, especially Maja Keech who supplied valuable information about slavery visuals, and the National Archives for locating the pictures for Lesson 17; my wife, who has supported me through this project, which has lasted now for 13 years from the beginning of writing the first version of Book 1 to this completion of the revised edition of Book 2.

INTRODUCTION

Thinking is what history is all about, as we try to more fully understand our past and thereby ourselves. We don't have many answers in history. Instead, we search for the truth, always attempting to get closer to what really happened. This book is meant to give you a taste of the excitement of historical interpretation and debate. It is also meant to give you guidance in learning the skills necessary to evaluate conflicting viewpoints. The goal is to empower you, as citizens in a democratic society, to make decisions for yourself regarding what you read, see, or hear about the issues of tomorrow—issues where there are few easy answers, and where reasonable people disagree.

This book is about historical interpretations or viewpoints. It is not itself a history book, but rather a series of situations on which historians present differing opinions. The purpose of this book is to teach you how to analyze and evaluate historical arguments.

If you think of a social, political, or economic issue today, you'll realize that people approach problems with different viewpoints. For example, reasonable people disagree about how much money should be spent on social welfare programs, about how to fight crime, and about the best candidate in an election. Historians also disagree about many events in history. Just as there are different ways to tell a fictional story, so there are many ways to tell the story of history. Historians, depending upon their backgrounds and frames of reference, select different information as important or unimportant.

The root word of history is story. As a "story," history seeks to explain past events. Why did a particular event happen when it did? How did a particular person or group of people affect the world around them? What underlying forces shaped events? Good historians have taken the time to step back, to carefully examine events to see the whole picture more clearly, to explain events more fully, and, thereby, to help our understanding of the world.

There are two broad kinds of history: analytical and narrative. In analytical history a historian makes a strong argument about an issue. The thesis is obvious, and the rest of the interpretation consists of a series of arguments to support the thesis. You probably have written thesis/support arguments in your English or social studies classes.

The second kind of history is narrative. Here, the historian tells a story, usually in chronological order. The various elements of the situation—economic forces, technological changes, social institutions, personalities, and so forth—are brought together as the drama unfolds. The main argument or thesis is not always obvious in narrative history. It has to be inferred from the way the story is told. Nevertheless, narrative history also contains a point of view or a thesis about why events happened the way they did.

This book presents both analytical and narrative history. For example, the interpretations on slavery in Lesson 16 are narrative; the interpretations in Lesson 14 are analytical; most are a combination of both.

One of the most important goals of this book is to introduce you to the conflicting viewpoints or interpretations of history. Ideally, you would read various historical interpretations of events, some of which are listed on pages 187–91. Realistically, you don't have the time to read all of these historical works. So this book contains short summaries of the interpretations. In some cases 300-page books have been summarized into one or two pages. Since this isn't fair to the original historians, their names have been replaced by titles: Historian A, Historian B, and so forth.

In some lessons the viewpoints are entitled Interpretation A or Theory A, rather than Historian A. Interpretation or Theory is used when no particular historian is identified with that point of view. These terms are also used to convey the idea that you should be forming your own interpretations or theories. The dictionary defines interpretation as "an explanation of what is not immediately plain or obvious," and it defines theory as "a judgment based on evidence or analysis." Ask your science teacher how the term *theory* is defined in science.

While most arguments presented in this book are those expressed by historians, a few are from historical participants. Thus, there are arguments by George Fitzhugh and Theodore Weld on slavery (Lesson 14).

This student book is comprised of three components:

Guide to Critical Thinking explains the parts of an argument and how to evaluate those parts.

Worksheets provide practice in the skills necessary for evaluating and constructing arguments.

Historical interpretation problems provide the opportunity for you to analyze historical arguments and make up your own mind.

Lessons within the book are arranged into three units: New Republic (Lessons 1–9), Slavery (Lessons 10–18), and Civil War (Lessons 19–27).

Thirteen of the lessons (#1–5, 10–13, and 19–22) are short worksheet lessons which focus on practicing particular skills. The other fourteen lessons (#6–9, 14–18, and 23–27) are longer historical interpretation problems where the skills can be applied.

UNIT 1
Guide to Critical Thinking

Purpose of This Unit

This Guide is meant to help you improve your critical thinking skills. Critical thinking, as used in this book, means evaluating or judging arguments. The critical thinker asks, "Why should I believe this?" or "How do I know this is true?" Just as importantly, critical thinking means constructing good arguments. Here, the critical thinker asks, "Why do I believe this?" and "Do I have a logical, well-supported case to back up my claims?"

As mentioned in the Introduction to this text, you are going to be confronted in this book with opposing viewpoints. You will have to decide for yourself which are stronger and which are weaker. This Guide will help you with the critical thinking skills necessary to judge the viewpoints presented and to express your own verbal and written views on topics.

Historians use critical thinking skills constantly in evaluating the reliability of documents, in selecting what is important, and in determining the underlying causes for events. But critical thinking is useful in everyday life as well. It is called for in such situations as buying a car, watching the news, voting, or deciding on a job or career. Improved skills in this area will help you make better judgments more often.

You can get an overall picture of critical thinking by reading through this Guide. You will find it most useful, however, when you need to use a particular skill in a particular lesson. For example, the section on evaluating **Generalizations** will be useful in Lesson 9, which asks several questions on recognizing and drawing good generalizations.

When Is an Argument Not a Fight?

An *argument* or interpretation, as used in this Guide, refers to presenting a conclusion and defending it with reasons that logically lead to the conclusion. You will have to decide for yourself how strong each argument is. A *case* is a set of arguments. The strength of a case may be judged by examining individual arguments. Arguments or interpretations may include any or all of the following components.

• Assertions • Evidence • Reasoning •
• Assumptions • Values•

Keep the importance of words in mind as you look through the following pages. Words are the keys to arguments. Signal words like "but," "however," and "on the other hand" indicate a change of direction in an argument. Words will serve as your clues in identifying parts of an argument and, once the argument has been identified, they will serve as your keys in analyzing the strength of that argument.

Once you recognize an argument, you will want to analyze it. You will break it down into its respective parts and evaluate the elements against certain standards of excellence in reasoning and evidence. You will examine the assumptions to see if they are warranted. You will consider how the author's values shape the evidence and reasoning presented.

Assertions

An assertion is a statement, conclusion, main point, or claim concerning an issue, person, or idea. It can be the conclusion of a very short argument, or it can be the main point (thesis) of an argument of perhaps two or more paragraphs.

For example, consider the short argument, "Bob is very responsible, so I'm sure he'll show up." The conclusion (assertion) in the argument is the phrase "...so I'm sure he'll show up." (The part of the argument that isn't the conclusion ["Bob is very responsible,..."] is called the premise. Premises are assumptions or reasons offered to support a conclusion. See the section on **Assumptions**, pages 15–16.)

Identifying Assertions

Words that often cue an assertion or conclusion include "therefore," "then," "so," and "thus." You can also identify an assertion by asking yourself, "What is the author trying to prove? Of what is the author trying to convince me?"

Evaluating Assertions

Two important questions to ask to evaluate the overall assertion of an argument are:

- Is the assertion supported by good reasons (supporting arguments)?
- Are the reasons supported by evidence?

Evidence

Evidence consists of the information a person uses to support assertions. It is the data, information, and knowledge which a historian, social scientist, or any communicator uses to support an argument; it is not the argument or interpretation itself.

There are many sources of evidence. Some of the more common sources include statements by witnesses or other people, written documents, objects, photographs, and video recordings. Lack of sources for evidence seriously weakens an argument. That is why many historical works include footnotes to cite sources; that is also why you should cite sources in essays you write.

For example, historians studying a Civil War battle could gather written accounts of the battle from sources such as diaries, battle reports, and letters. They could examine objects that had been found on the battlefield and photographs taken at the time of the battle. They also might use accounts by other historians, but these would be weaker sources because they are not eyewitness accounts (see primary sources below).

IDENTIFYING EVIDENCE

To help locate evidence in an argument, look for endnotes, quotation marks, or such words as "according to," "so-and-so said," or "such-and-such shows."

The initial questions to be asked when evaluating any evidence offered in support of an argument should be:

- Is there a source given for this information?
- If so, what is it?

EVALUATING EVIDENCE

Only when you know the sources of evidence can you judge how reliable the evidence actually is. Frequently, you can use the following evaluation method when considering evidence and its sources. This can be shortened to **PROP**; remember that good sources will "prop up" evidence.

P Is it a primary (eyewitness) or secondary (not an eyewitness) source?

Primary sources are invariably more desirable. To reach valid conclusions, you need to realize the importance of primary sources and gather as many as possible to use as evidence in an argument. You should depend on secondary sources, like encyclopedias or history texts, only when primary sources are unavailable.

R If the source is a person, does he or she have any reason to distort the evidence?

Would those giving the statement, writing the document, recording the audio (or video), or identifying the object benefit if the truth were distorted, covered up, falsified, sensationalized, or manipulated? Witnesses with no reason to distort the evidence are more desirable than those who might benefit from a particular presentation of the evidence.

O Are there other witnesses, statements, recordings, or evidence which report the same data, information, or knowledge?

Having other evidence verify the initial evidence strengthens the argument.

P Is it a public or private statement?

If the person making the statement of evidence knew or intended that other people should hear it, then it is a public statement. A private statement may be judged more accurate because it was probably said in confidence and is, therefore, more likely to reflect the speaker's true feelings or observations.

These four factors (**PROP**) will be enough to evaluate most evidence you encounter. Additional factors that are sometimes considered regarding evidence include:

Witnesses

- What are the frames of reference (points of view) of the witnesses? What are their values? What are their backgrounds?
- Are the witnesses expert (recognized authorities) on what they saw?
- Did the witnesses believe their statements could be checked? (If I believe you can check my story with other witnesses, I am more likely to tell the truth.)
- Was what the witnesses said an observation ("Maria smiled") or an inference ("Maria was happy")? Inferences are judgments that can reveal much about the witnesses' points of view or motives (reasons) for making statements.

Observation Conditions

- Were physical conditions conducive to witnessing the event? (Was it foggy? Noisy? Dark?)
- What were the physical locations of the witnesses in relation to the event? Were they close to the action? Was there anything blocking their view?

Witnesses' Statement or Document

- Is the document authentic or a forgery?
- What is the reputation of the source containing the document?
- How soon after the event was the statement made?
- Did the witnesses use precise techniques or tools to report or record the event? For example, did they take notes or use reference points?

Reasoning

Just as evidence can be judged for its reliability, so reasoning can be evaluated for its logic.

Reasoning is the logical process through which a person reaches conclusions. For example, you notice that the car is in the driveway (evidence) so you reason that your mother is home (conclusion). Five kinds of reasoning are frequently used in historical interpretations:

- cause and effect
- comparison
- generalization
- proof (by evidence, example, or authority)
- debating (eliminating alternatives)

These types of reasoning, along with questions to help evaluate them and fallacies (errors in reasoning) for each, are explained below.

Reasoning by Cause and Effect

This type of reasoning is used when someone argues that something caused, brought about, or will result in something else. For example, Laura's motorcycle will not start (effect), so she decides it must be out of gas (proposed cause).

Causation is very complex—so complex that some historians feel that they do not really understand the causes of an event even after years of study. Other historians do not even use the word cause; instead they talk about change. Please keep a sense of humility when you study causation. When you finish your course, you are not going to know all the causes of complex events. Rather, you are going to know a little bit more about how to sort out causes.

Historians believe in multiple causation, that is, that every event has several or many causes. This belief does not, however, relieve us of the responsibility of trying to figure out which are the most important causes. Indeed, one of the most frequent sources of debate among historians stems from disagreements over the main causes of events.

Identifying Cause-and-Effect Reasoning

One way to identify cause-and-effect reasoning is to watch for such cue words as "caused," "led to," "forced," "because," "brought about," "resulted in," or "reason for." You can also identify it by asking, "Is the author arguing that one thing resulted from another?"

Evaluating Cause-and-Effect Reasoning

Several important questions may be used to evaluate the strength of a causal explanation.

- Is there a **reasonable connection** between the cause and the effect? Does the arguer state the connection?

  In the motorcycle example, for instance, there is a reasonable connection between the motorcycle being out of gas and not starting. Lack of gasoline would cause a motorcycle not to start.

- Might there be **other possible causes** for this effect? Has the arguer eliminated these as possible causes?

  There are also, however, other possible causes for a motorcycle failing to start. Maybe the starter isn't working. Other possible causes have not been eliminated.

- Might there be **important previous causes** that led to the proposed cause?

  In some cases a previous cause might be more important than the proposed cause; e.g., a leak in the gasoline tank might cause a motorcycle to be out of gasoline. In this case simply putting gasoline in the tank will not make the engine run again.

Cause-and-Effect Fallacies

Single cause

Any conclusion that a historical event had but one cause commits the single-cause fallacy. For example, the statements "Eloise married Jon because he's handsome" and "Antiwar protest caused the United States to pull out of the Vietnam War" both make use of the single-cause fallacy.

In both cases there are likely to be other factors, or causes, involved. The fallacy can be avoided by carefully investigating and explaining the complexity of causes. Be careful, however. Historians may sometimes assert that something "caused" an event when they really mean it was the main, not the only, cause.

Preceding event as cause

A Latin phrase (*Post hoc, ergo propter hoc*), meaning "after this, therefore because of this," is the technical name of a fallacy that occurs when someone assumes that because event B happened after event A, A caused B. "I washed my car, so naturally it rained" and "Since the Depression followed the stock market crash of 1929, the stock market crash must have caused it" are both examples of this fallacy. To avoid the error, the author of the argument must explain how A caused B.

Correlation as cause

This fallacy occurs when a conclusion is reached that because A and B occurred at the same time or occur regularly at the same time (the correlation), then one caused the other.

Some correlations, such as cigarette smoking and increased incidence of heart disease, are very strong. Others are not as strong. In some correlations where A is argued to cause B, ask yourself if B could instead have caused A. For example, "Students who have fewer absences (A) achieve higher grades in school (B)." In this case, consideration might also be given to the correlation that "Students who achieve higher grades in school (B) have fewer absences (A)."

Again, the fallacy might be avoided by an explanation of how A caused B. Since, however, a connection cannot always be shown, people are frequently forced to rely on correlations. For example, you don't have to know, mechanically, *how* a car works to know that turning the ignition should cause it to start.

False scenario

This fallacy uses the argument that if something had happened, then something else would have happened (or if something had not happened, then something else would not have happened). "If you hadn't told Mother on me, I wouldn't be in trouble" is an example of false-scenario reasoning. "If we had not built railroads in the late 1800s, the United States would not have had as much economic growth as it did with the railroads" is another.

Although some of this kind of predicting can occur when we have a great deal of evidence regarding what might have happened, it is generally much less certain than causal reasoning about what actually did happen. To avoid this fallacy, concern yourself with what actually happened rather than what might have happened.

Reasoning by Comparison

This type of reasoning, sometimes called "reasoning by analogy," consists of two basic types, both of which involve drawing comparisons between two cases.

Alike comparison

The first type of comparison chooses two cases (people, events, objects, etc.) and reasons that since they are alike in some ways, they will be alike in some other way. For example, Joe might reason that Fernandez did all of his homework and got an "A" in geometry, so if Joe does all of his homework he can also get an "A." Joe is reasoning that since the two cases (his and Fernandez's) are similar in terms of homework (doing it all), they will be similar in terms of outcome (an "A").

Difference comparison

The second type compares two cases and reasons that since they are different in some respect, something must be true. For example, Juan might reason that his baseball team is better than Cleon's, since Juan's team won more games. Juan is concluding that since the two cases (teams) are different in some respect (one team won more games), it is true that the team that won the most games is a better team.

If Joe and Fernandez are taking the same course (geometry), and have the same mathematical ability and the same teacher, then the conclusion that the outcome would be the same is stronger than it would be if they were different in any or all of these areas. If the two baseball teams played the same opponents and the same number of games, then the conclusion that one team is better (different) than the other is stronger than it would be if they were different in any of these ways.

Usually, more similarities make a stronger argument. A similarity found in an argument of difference, however, will weaken the argument. If the two baseball teams had the same winning percentage, then the conclusion that one was better (different) than the other would be weakened by this similarity.

As another example of a difference comparison, examine the argument: "The federal budget deficit increased from $800 billion three years ago to $912 billion this year. We've got to do something about it before it destroys our economy." What if the federal budget deficit were 4% of the Gross National

Product (the measure of goods and services produced in a year) three years ago and 4% this year also? Here, a similarity found between the deficits of the two years being compared weakens the conclusion that the federal budget deficit is getting worse. Thus, differences weaken arguments comparing similarities, and similarities weaken arguments comparing differences.

IDENTIFYING COMPARISON REASONING

Cue words can help identify comparisons. Watch for such comparative terms as "like," "similar to," "same as," "greater (or less) than," "better (or worse) than," and "increased (or decreased)." Some comparisons, however, are implied rather than stated. For example, someone might say, "Oh, I wouldn't travel by plane. It's too dangerous." You might ask "dangerous compared to what?" If a higher percentage of people are injured or killed using alternate methods of travel (automobiles, trains), then the statement is weakened considerably.

In examining comparisons, ask yourself:

- How are the cases similar; how are they different?

EVALUATING COMPARISON REASONING

This skill involves *evaluating comparison arguments*. It is not the same activity as "compare and contrast," where you are asked to find the similarities and differences between two items; i.e., "Compare and contrast the American and French Revolutions." In evaluating comparison arguments you, on your own, are to recognize that a comparison argument is being made and, without being told, ask about the similarities and differences of the two cases being compared.

Reasoning by Generalization

This kind of reasoning includes both definitional and statistical generalizations. The generalization, "No U.S. senator is under 30 years of age," is an example of a *definitional generalization*, since by legal definition, a United States senator must be at least 30 years of age.

Statistical generalization is important to evaluating historical arguments. Statistical generalizations argue that what is true for some (part or sample) of a group (such as wars, women, or songs) will be true in roughly the same way for all of the group. For example, Maribeth might argue that since the bite of pizza she took (sample) is cold, the whole pizza (the whole group) is cold.

Statistical generalizations can be further subdivided into two types. *Hard generalizations* are those applied to all (or none) of the members of a group, e.g., the whole cold pizza above, or a statement like "All the apples have fallen off the tree." A hard generalization is disproved by one counterexample (contrary case). For example, if there is one apple still on the tree, the generalization is disproved.

Soft generalizations are those applied to most (or few) members of a group, e.g., "Most people remember the Vietnam War." A soft generalization is not disproved by one—or even several—contrary cases, but the generalization is weakened as the contrary cases add up. For example, if someone says that Luis does not remember the Vietnam War, the generalization is not disproved. If, however, that person cites fifty people who do not remember the Vietnam War, the generalization is getting shaky.

The probability that a statistical generalization is correct increases with the size of the sample and the degree to which a sample is representative of the whole group. Your generalization that "Nella is prompt" is more likely to be accurate if she was on time on all twenty occasions when she was supposed to meet you than if she was on time the only time she was supposed to meet you.

Representativeness is even more important than size in generalizations. In the pizza example the sample is quite small (only one bite from the whole pizza) but very representative—if one part of the pizza is cold, it is highly likely that the whole pizza is cold. Similarly, presidential election polls are small (about 1200 people polled) but usually very accurate, since those sampled are quite representative of the whole electorate. If you think of the whole group of voters as a circle, a presidential election poll might look like Figure 1.

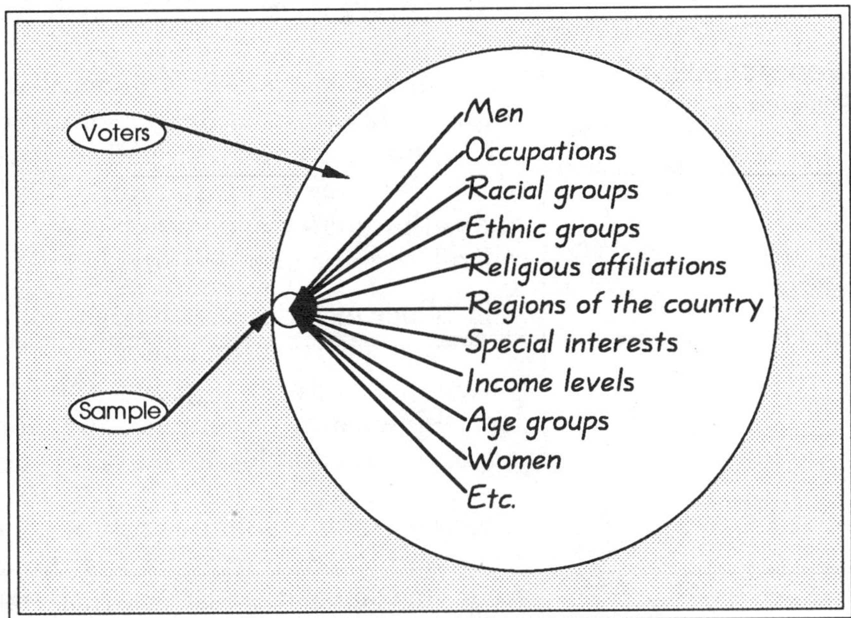

Figure 1. The sample should represent all these groups of voters (and many more) in the same proportion as they make up the whole electorate.

Identifying Generalizations

You can recognize statistical generalizations by watching for their cue words ("all," "none," "some," "most," "a majority," "few") or plural nouns ("women," "farmers," or "people").

EVALUATING GENERALIZATIONS

Questions you should ask when evaluating generalizations include the following.

- How large is the sample?
  The strength of a statistical generalization is improved by larger sized sampling.
- How representative is the sample?
  If you picture the generalization as a little circle and a big circle, as in Figure 1, the question becomes: Does the little circle have all the same subgroups in the same proportion as the big circle?

You should not, however, be concerned only with evaluating generalizations that other people make. You should also be concerned with how far you can legitimately generalize from what you know.

For example, if you learned that slaves on ten large cotton plantations in Maryland in the 1850s were brutally treated, you might generalize that slaves on most large cotton plantations in Maryland at that time were brutally treated. You would be on much shakier ground, however, to generalize that slaves on most plantations were brutally treated at all times. You really have no information about slaves on, say, small Virginia tobacco plantations in the 1720s, so you shouldn't make such a broad generalization. The warning is, "Do not overgeneralize."

Generalization Fallacies

Hasty generalization

This fallacy consists of a general conclusion based on an inappropriately small or unrepresentative sample. For example, suppose a reporter polls three people in Illinois, all of whom say they support gun control. If the reporter concludes that all (or even most) people in Illinois support gun control, then he or she is making a hasty generalization.

This fallacy includes such oversimplifications as "If it weren't for bankers, we wouldn't have wars." To avoid such fallacies, remember that any group (such as people, wars, or depressions) is quite complex and must be carefully sampled to take those complexities into account.

Composition and division (stereotyping)

These two related fallacies confuse the characteristics of the group and the characteristics of the individuals within that group. In composition, the characteristics of the individual(s) within the group are ascribed (given) to the whole group. ("She's a good lawyer, so the law firm she is a member of must be a good firm.") In division, characteristics that belong to the group as a whole are assumed to belong to each of the individuals. ("She's a member of a good law firm, so she must be a good lawyer.")

These fallacies are commonly referred to as *stereotyping*, which is defined as "applying preconceived ideas to a group or members of a group." This results in the groups or individuals being judged before we really know them. This act of prejudging is where we derive the word *prejudice*. "You're Jewish, so you must be well educated" and "Of course he's a drinker, he's Irish!" are examples of stereotype statements.

Special pleading

In this fallacy the arguer presents a conclusion based on information favorable to the argument while ignoring unfavorable information. ("Mom, I should be able to go to the dance. I passed my history test and got an 'A' in math." [...omitting the information that I failed science and English.]) A good argument avoids this fallacy by including unfavorable information and overcoming it with compelling reasons for accepting the thesis or conclusion.

Reasoning by Proof (Evidence, Example, or Authority)

These types of reasoning concern whether or not the evidence or authority used supports the point being argued. It does not concern the strengths and weakness of the evidence itself (see the **Evidence** section of the Guide). Similarly, the word "proof" as used here does not mean absolute proof—as in mathematics—but rather refers to methods used to support an argument or interpretation.

This is generally a legitimate method of supporting an argument. For example, a doctor might be called to testify in court to support the argument that a claimant had certain injuries (proof by authority). A biologist might explain the results of several investigations (example), cite evidence gathered (evidence), and quote the written opinions of several experts (authority) to support an argument on the effects of toxic waste.

Identifying Proof Reasoning

Proof reasoning can be identified by cue words such as "for example," "for instance," "according to," "authority," and "expert." When evaluating argument by proof, you should look at the answers to several questions:

Evaluating Proof

Evidence

- Does the evidence prove the point being argued? Does it support the point under consideration?

Examples

- Are the examples pertinent to the argument?

Authority

- Is this person an expert on this particular topic? What are the qualifications of the authority? Are they presented?
- Do other authorities agree with these conclusions? Are there any authorities who disagree with the conclusion? Are counterarguments acknowledged and/or refuted?

Fallacies of Proof

Irrelevant proof

Arguments which present compelling evidence that does not apply to the argument in question are fallacies of irrelevant proof. For example, "If you flunk me, I'll lose my scholarship" and "Everyone else does it" are fallacies of irrelevant proof. As a further example, suppose Senator Smith is accused of taking bribes to vote for certain laws and, in his defense, presents a great deal of evidence that shows he is a good family man. This evidence does not concern his actions as a senator and is thus irrelevant to the charges. Good arguments avoid this fallacy by sticking to the issue under question.

Negative proof

This fallacy type presents a conclusion based on the lack or absence of evidence to the contrary. For example, "There is no evidence that Senator Macklem is an honest woman, so it's obvious she is a crook" or "Since you haven't proven that there is no Santa Claus, there must be one." Remember that you must present evidence to **support** your conclusions when you are making a case.

Prevalent proof

Related to the fallacy of negative proof, this fallacy concludes that something must be the case because "everyone knows" it is the case. Such arguments as "Everyone knows she's a winner" and "Politicians can't be trusted; everyone knows that" are examples of the prevalent proof fallacy. Remember, in previous times "everyone knew" that the sun revolved around the earth! The critical thinker sometimes asks questions even about things which everyone knows.

Numbers

A conclusion that the argument is right solely because of the great amount of evidence gathered commits the fallacy of numbers. For example, "We checked hundreds of thousands of government records, so our theory must be right."

Notice that no mention is made of what the "government records" contained—the argument only states that they were "checked." A great deal of evidence can be amassed to support a slanted perspective or an argument using poor reasoning or faulty assumptions. When constructing arguments, check them not only for strong evidence but also for sound reasoning and assumptions.

Appeal to authority

A conclusion that is based only on the statement of an expert commits the appeal-to-authority fallacy. Such arguments conclude, "I'm right because I'm an expert" and lack additional supporting evidence. For example, the argument "It must be true because it says so right here in the book" is based only on the "authority" of the book's author. Arguments must be judged on the strength of their evidence and their reasoning rather than solely on the authority of their authors.

Appeal to the golden mean

This logical fallacy is committed when the argument is made that the conclusion is right because it is moderate (between the extreme views). If someone argued, "Some people say Adolf Hitler was right in what he did, while others say he was one of the most evil leaders in history. These views are so extreme that a more moderate view must be right. He must have been an average leader," he or she would be appealing to the golden mean. (Of course, the "extreme" view that Hitler was evil is right in this case.)

This fallacy can be avoided by realizing that there is no reason for an extreme view to be wrong simply because it is extreme. At one time it was considered "extreme" to think that women should vote or that people would fly.

Reasoning by Debate (eliminating alternatives)

Reasoning by debate helps a person see why one interpretation should be believed over other interpretations and puts an interpretation into a context. It is not surprising, therefore, that articles in historical journals frequently begin by a survey of other interpretations of the topic under study and an attempt to refute opposing interpretations.

This type of reasoning advances an argument by referring to and attempting to show the weaknesses of alternative interpretations. This attempt to disprove, called debating, is not only acceptable, but desirable. For example, someone might argue, "Peter thinks Mi-Ling will get the lead role in the play, but he's wrong. Lucetta has a better voice and more acting experience, so she'll get the lead." A historian might argue, "Although the traditional view is that slavery is the main cause of the Civil War, people who hold that view are wrong. Economic problems, especially over the tariff, were the main cause of the bloody war." Both are applying reasoning by debate.

IDENTIFYING DEBATES

Cue words for this type of reasoning include "other people believe," "the traditional view is," "other views are wrong because," "older interpretations," and "other viewpoints are."

EVALUATING DEBATES

To help evaluate debate reasoning, ask questions like the following.

- Have all reasonable alternatives been considered? Have they all been eliminated as possibilities?
- Does this author attack the other views in a fair way?
- What might the authors of the other views say in response to this argument?

In eliminating possible alternatives, the author must be careful to attack the argument rather than the arguer, to present reasoned evidence against the argument, and to fairly interpret the alternative argument under consideration. This form of questioning can also be helpful when there is a lack of information.

Fallacies of Debate

Either-or

This fallacy presents a conclusion that since A and B were the only possible explanations—and since A was not possible, B is proven to be the explanation. For example, "Only Willis and Cross were around, but Willis was swimming so Cross must have done it." What if someone else was actually around but no one saw him or her?

Of course, eliminating alternatives can be very important to reasoning a problem through, as Sherlock Holmes demonstrates so well. But one must be careful to ask: Have all alternatives been eliminated? Could it be both alternatives? Don't let yourself be "boxed in" by this type of reasoning.

Attacking the arguer

(In logical terminology, this is called *ad hominem*–Latin for "to the man.") This fallacy occurs when statements are directed at the person making the argument rather than at the arguments presented. For example, the statement "No one should listen to what Mrs. Rouge says. She's a Communist" is an attack on Mrs. Rouge personally rather than on the statement she made.

Sometimes the attack is more subtle, such as a look of disgust, a negative comment ("I don't believe you just said that"), or sarcastic laughter. Good arguments avoid this fallacy by refuting the argument, not the person.

Straw man

This is the technique of attacking the opponents' argument by adding to or changing what a person said, then attacking the additions or changes. For example, Johannas says he's opposed to capital punishment, and Thibedeau replies, "People like you who oppose punishing criminals make me sick." (Johannas did not say he opposed punishing criminals.) When constructing an argument, remember to be fair and argue against what your opponents said, not your version of what they said.

There are many methods of trying to prove something. The types of reasoning explained above (cause and effect; comparisons; generalizations; proof by evidence, example, or authority; and debate) are all methods of proof to be considered when evaluating historical arguments. The next section examines assumptions, which are like reasoning in that they lead to conclusions (assertions). They are different from reasoning, however, in that they are not always consciously argued. Authors frequently do not realize the assumptions they are making.

Assumptions

An assumption is the part of an argument containing the ideas or opinions that the arguer takes for granted. Stated assumptions are not of concern for the purposes of this Guide. When authors say they are assuming something, all you decide is whether you agree with the stated assumption.

Unstated assumptions are more difficult to recognize. There are two types of unstated assumptions: the general, more encompassing type and the specific type.

General Unstated Assumptions

These assumptions are part of the argument as a whole and, as such, cannot be identified by rewriting particular arguments. In any argument there are an infinite number of such assumptions. For example, if you say you are going to the store to buy a TV, you are making the general assumptions that the store will be there, that you won't die on the way, that they'll have televisions in stock, and so forth. Some assumptions are trivial or unlikely, but others are very important. For example, if the President of the United States says, "We will not agree to the Soviet proposal to have both countries eliminate half of their missiles because we cannot check on them adequately," he is assuming the Soviets cannot be trusted. If, on the other hand, the President agreed to missile reductions without a means of verifying Soviet reductions, he would then be assuming the Soviets can be trusted. He might or might not be right in either case. The important point is that we should recognize his assumption.

General assumptions shape historical interpretations. A historian who assumes that economics drives people's behavior will select economic information and write from that perspective; a historian who assumes that politics, in the form of power and compromise, shapes society will focus on that area in both research and writing.

Specific Unstated Assumptions

To understand specific unstated assumptions you need to know something about the form of arguments. As was explained in the section on **Assertions**, arguments are made up of the conclusion and the rest of the argument, which is designed to prove the conclusion. The sentences that comprise the rest of the argument are called *premises*.

Short arguments take the form of *premise, premise, conclusion*. A well-known example is: "Socrates is a man. All men are mortal. Therefore, Socrates is mortal." In premise, premise, conclusion format, this would be:

Premise: Socrates is a man.
Premise: All men are mortal.
Conclusion: Therefore, Socrates is mortal.

If the above argument "looks funny," it's because people rarely talk this way. In normal speech, we often state the conclusion first: "I should be able to go outside now. My homework is done." It is also common to not state one of the premises or the conclusion at all. For example, if we are trying to decide who should pay for the broken vase, you might say, "Well, Joaquin pushed me into it." Your point (although you did not state it) is that Joaquin should pay.

When you leave out a premise, you are making an assumption. For example, the argument, "We should spend our vacation in the mountains because we need a rest," can be rewritten this way:

Premise: We need a rest.

Premise: ??

Conclusion: (Therefore) we should spend our vacation in the mountains.

The missing premise is the assumption.

IDENTIFYING ASSUMPTIONS

You can figure out what the assumption is by asking, "What has to be true for this conclusion to be true?" In the above case, the missing premise (assumption) is: "The mountains are a good place to rest."

EVALUATING ASSUMPTIONS

When you have identified an assumption, evaluate it by asking if the assumption is correct. Assumptions are frequently related to the beliefs and values of the author, as explained in the next section.

Values

Values are conditions that the person making an argument believes are important, worthwhile, or intrinsically good for themselves, their family, their country, and their world. Money, success, friendship, love, health, peace, power, freedom, and equality are examples of things people may value.

It is often important to discover the underlying values of the author of an argument, since assumptions made by an author are often related to the author's beliefs and values. This will help you understand why the viewpoint is argued the way it is, and, in cases where your values may be different from the author's values, it will help you understand why you might disagree with the argument. For example, if you believe that peace is more important than demonstrating power, then you are going to disagree with an argument which says that since Country A increased its power by attacking Country B; it was right to attack.

IDENTIFYING VALUE STATEMENTS

Clues to an author's value judgments are found in sentences containing words such as "good," "bad," "right," "wrong," "justified," "should," or "should not." For example, if someone says, "The United States was wrong (value judgment) to drop the atomic bomb on Hiroshima because so many people were killed," that person is saying that life (value) is more important than the other conditions or values involved (power, peace vs. war, etc.).

To help identify an author's values, ask:

- Who wrote this?
- What beliefs does this person hold?

When you have identified a value judgment in an argument, you can then examine it. For example, consider the argument, "We should have capital punishment because criminals will commit fewer crimes if they think they might be executed."

EVALUATING VALUE STATEMENTS

1. *Separate the argument into its factual and value parts.*

   Factual part:

   Capital punishment will make criminals commit fewer crimes. (Notice that this could be investigated by examining statistics on the number of crimes with and without capital punishment.)

   Value assumption:

   Fewer crimes is good (a desirable outcome).

2. *Rephrase the value statement into general terms.*

   Anything (general term) which causes fewer crimes is good (value judgment).

3. *Ask yourself if the value statement is right in all instances.*

   Is the statement, "Anything which causes fewer crimes is good" true? Can you think of cases in which you might not agree? Substitute some specific situations and see if the statement is still right. For example, "Jailing all people accused of a crime, whether found guilty or not, would also cause fewer crimes to be committed. Should we do this?"

This kind of questioning will help both you and the person who originally made the claim think more fully about the value(s) behind the claim.

Three general questions can be used to test the worthiness of value claims.

- Are you willing to use this value in all situations?
- What would society be like if everyone believed and acted on this value?
- Would you want the value applied to you?

The next page contains two charts you may find helpful for reminding you of methods you can use to analyze the viewpoints presented in this book. As you proceed, refer to this "Guide to Critical Thinking" to help you with the lessons.

A MODEL FOR ANALYZING ARGUMENTS

A model is a way of organizing information. One type of model is an acronym where each letter in the model stands for a word. The model outlined here is **ARMEAR**. Each letter will remind you of a part of arguments to examine.

A	**Author**	• Who wrote this interpretation and why? • What are the author's values or beliefs? • What can you learn about the author?
R	**Relevant Information**	• What do you know about the topic being argued or topics related to it?
M	**Main Point**	• What is the main point or thesis of the argument?
E	**Evidence**	• What evidence is presented to support the argument? • How reliable is it? • What are the sources of the evidence?
A	**Assumptions**	• What assumptions does the author make?
R	**Reasoning**	• What reasoning is used in the argument? Cause and effect? Comparison? Generalization? Proof? Debate? • How strong is the reasoning?

FIVE MAIN PARTS OF AN ARGUMENT

Assertion, main point, or thesis	• What is the author trying to prove?
Evidence	• Is the source given for information? • How strong is it? Primary? Reason to distort? Other evidence to verify? Public or private? (**PROP**).
Reasoning	• Cause and Effect — Is the connection shown? Are there other possible causes? Is there an important cause previous to the one proposed? • Comparisons — How are the two cases different and how are they similar? • Generalizations — How large and representative is the sample? • Proof — Does the evidence support the point being made? How many examples are given? Is this authority an expert on this topic? • Debate — Does the author attack other views in a fair way? Have all possible alternatives been eliminated?
Assumptions	• What must be true if the thesis is true (acceptable)?
Values	• Do I agree with these values? • Is this value position right in all instances?

UNIT 2
New Republic

LESSON 1 Identifying Sources

When someone makes a claim or states an opinion, we should require that person to give information (often examples), and tell us the source of the information. The source is the person, written document, or object from which the information came. The source may also be the person making the claim, based on his or her own observations or experiences.

> When evaluating claims or opinions you should ask the person
> - What information do you have to support your claims?
> - From what source do you get the information?

Q Label each item below with the appropriate letter.

S A **source** of information is given.

N **No** source of information is given.

_______1. In Canada legal abortions were done throughout pregnancy, according to a *Time* cover story of May 4, 1992.

_______2. "The Cosby Show" was very popular in the United States.

_______3. Farmers hated railroad tracks, which often ran diagonally across fields, creating triangular parcels to plow.

_______4. A Bank of the United States was chartered by Congress in February 1791.

_______5. Marcus Cunliffe says in his book, *The Nation Takes Shape*, that the countries of Europe in 1789 were too engrossed in the affairs of their own continent to pay much attention to the United States.

_______6. Yellow jackets were a major hazard for farmers plowing new fields. These wasps made their nests in the ground and swarmed when disturbed.

_______7. The diaries of Lewis and Clark describe the beautiful landscape of the Pacific Northwest.

_______8. The first turnpike in the United States was the Lancaster Turnpike, from Philadelphia to Pennsylvania Dutch country, which opened in 1791.[1]

[1] J. C. Furnas, *The Americans: A Social History of the United States, 1587–1914*, (New York: G. P. Putnam's Sons, 1969) p. 275.

LESSON 2 Evaluating Sources

Primary Sources

A primary source is evidence given (often in writing) by a person who was present at, or part of, the event reported. Or, it is an object that was part of the event.

> To determine the type of source, ask yourself:
>
> - Was the person or object present at the time of the event?
> - Did the person see the event on which she or he is reporting?
>
> If so, the source is a primary source.

Q Label each item below with the appropriate letter.

P It is a **primary** source.
S It is a **secondary** source.

_______1. Meghan said Bill's performance was the best she'd seen this year.

_______2. Historian Marcus Cunliffe said in his book, *The Nation Takes Shape*, that while Europeans were inventive of mechanical equipment, Americans were excellent at making improvements and modifications to it.

_______3. In his travel accounts, Zebulon Pike described the areas he explored as dry, treeless, and unsuitable for American farmers.

_______4. A Currier and Ives painting showed a railway train in a very positive way—clean, sleek, and exciting.

_______5. A Boston newspaper account in 1849 reported the gold rush in California.

Reason to Lie

People have a reason to lie when they make themselves or their group look good or

[Continued on next page.]

[Continued from previous page.]

when they help their own interests (for example, when they make more money). People generally have no reason to lie when they (often without realizing it) make themselves look bad or their enemy look good.

Q Label each item below with the appropriate letter.

R The person has a **reason** to lie.

N The person has **no** reason to lie.

_______6. Rita told the coach that she missed practice because she was sick.

_______7. President Madison, in a speech in June 1812, asked Congress to declare war on Britain because of British violations of American rights on the sea.

_______8. George Washington, in his Farewell Address to the nation at the end of his presidency, argued that the United States should stay out of alliances and conflicts, especially in Europe.

_______9. Congressman Feliz Grundy of Tennessee argued in 1811 that the British had hurt the United States, so we had a duty to fight them.

_____10. The census of 1830 showed that the population had increased significantly since 1800.

Corroboration

Corroboration means finding other evidence to support evidence you already have. If I claim that Bill was a great baseball player and you find a newspaper article saying that Bill was a great baseball player, you have corroborated what I said. What evidence would you search for to corroborate the evidence in the following?

11. Question #3 (p. 20)

12. Question #7 (above)

LESSON 3 Determining Causes and Effects

- An **effect** is an event or situation which results from something.
- A **cause** is a reason for a result, or it is something which brings about an effect.

Q Label the items in each group below with the appropriate letter. (The first one is done for you as an example.)

C This portion of the statement is the **cause**.
E This portion of the statement is the **effect**.

C 1. Since it was supposed to rain on Tuesday,

E 2. we decided not to go to the park.

_______3. The tires are worn down unevenly

_______4. because the car is out of line.

_______5. Roads were very poor in the United States in the early 1800s,

_______6. so the federal government began to build national roads.

_______7. Canals were built later than roads

_______8. due to their greater cost to build.

[Continued on next page.]

[Continued from previous page.]

In order to be cause-and-effect reasoning the statement has to argue that something caused, led to, or brought about something else.

Q Label each item below with the appropriate letter. If cause-and-effect reasoning is shown in the argument, identify the cause and the effect in the space provided below each item.

C Item uses **cause-and-effect** reasoning.

N Item does **not** use cause-and-effect reasoning.

_______9. The Hillcrest Steak House is the busiest restaurant in the area.

CAUSE: EFFECT:

_____10. The supply of wheat is smaller because of the drought in the Midwest.

CAUSE: EFFECT:

_____11. Fur trapping depleted fur-bearing animals in some eastern areas by 1700, so in the next fifty years, trappers pushed 1000 miles inland, far in advance of European settlement.

CAUSE: EFFECT:

_____12. In 1804–1805, Lewis and Clark explored a large part of the Louisiana Purchase, all the way to the Pacific Ocean.

CAUSE: EFFECT:

LESSON 4 Evaluating Cause-and-Effect Reasoning

The section on **Cause-and-Effect Reasoning** in the "Guide to Critical Thinking" (Unit 1) explains that one question you should ask of any cause-and-effect argument is, "Is there a connection between the cause and the effect?" This part of the lesson focuses on assessing the strengths of connections between causes and effects.

Label each item below with the appropriate letter, then explain your answer in the space provided.

S There is a **strong** connection between the cause and the effect.

R There may be a **reasonable** connection between the cause and the effect, but it is not explained well in this argument.

W There is a **weak** connection between the cause and the effect.

_______1. On a whole, people who watch more violence on television are more violent than people who do not.

_______2. As railroad speeds increased in the United States in the mid-1800s, the severity of accidents increased to match.

_______3. American farmers who practiced a field-rotation system, which replenished land and nutrients, got more yield per acre than those farmers who did not.

Q Another question you should ask in evaluating cause-and-effect arguments is "Are there other possible causes than the one proposed for this effect?" This section focuses on other causes. For each of the following items, think of as many possible causes as you can, then evaluate the strength of the argument given.

4. Why do girls sometimes break up with their boyfriends? List all the reasons you can think of.

John told Peter: "Alyssa broke up with me because I didn't ask her to go to the prom."

How strong do you think this explanation is? Support your opinion.

[Continued on next page.]

[Continued from previous page.]

5. What are the reasons why a country might go to war with another country? List all the reasons you can think of.

"The Mexican War was caused chiefly by American expansion in the 1840s. President Polk's desire for land from Mexico and his insistence on the Rio Grande boundary upset the Mexican government, excited American public opinion, and led directly to the conflict."

How strong do you think the above explanation is? Support your opinion.

Q This section focuses on both questions for evaluating cause-and-effect arguments: "Is there a strong connection between cause and effect?" and "Are there other possible causes?" Fill in the diagram for each cause-and-effect argument below, then use the information from the diagram to evaluate the strength of the argument.

6. Naturally the Blue Jays (baseball team) raised ticket prices this year. Last season the team won the pennant, so people should be willing to pay more to see them play.

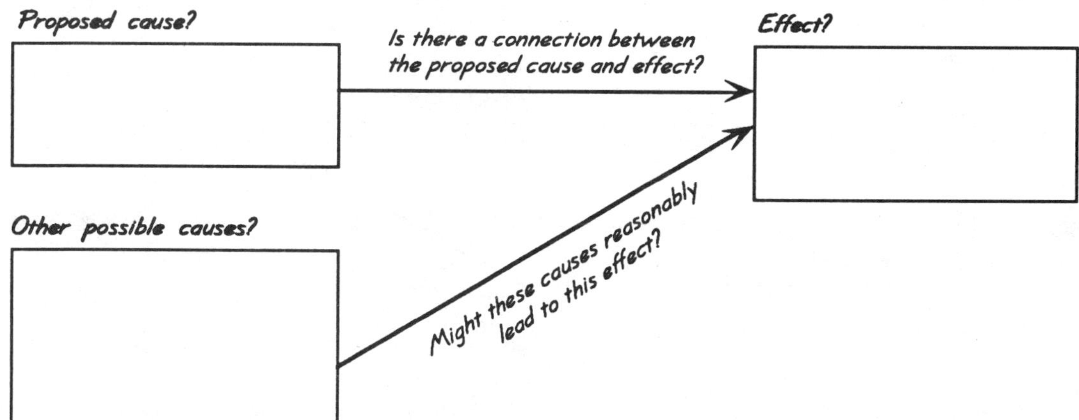

How strong is this argument? Why do you think so?

[Continued on next page.]

[Continued from previous page.]

7. Plains Indians were dependent on the buffalo for their way of life. The buffalo furnished Indians with food, clothing, a home, traditions, and even religious meaning. So when white men wiped out the buffalo, they also destroyed the Plains Indians' way of life.

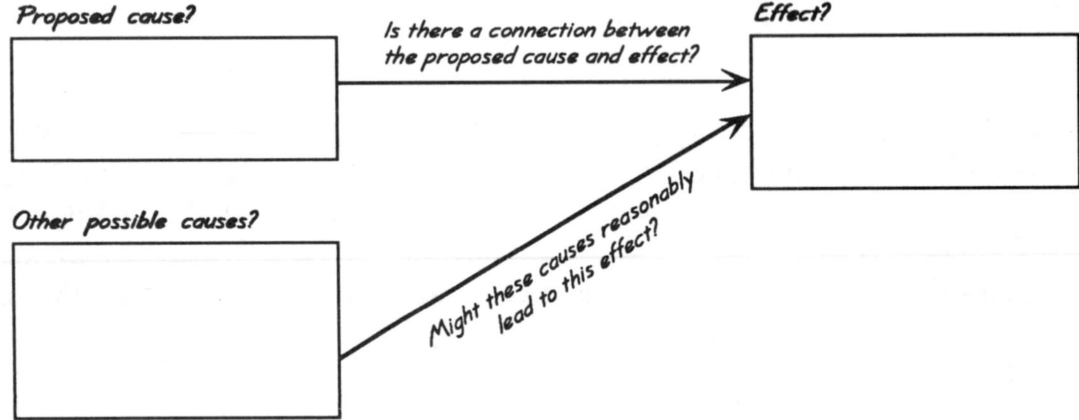

How strong is this argument? Why do you think so?

8. When the silk topper replaced the beaver hat as the fashionable head wear in Europe in the 1830s, the era of the mountain man (fur trapper) was at an end. The main, almost only, use of beaver pelts was for hats. Beaver pelts were no longer profitable, so trappers had to find other work.

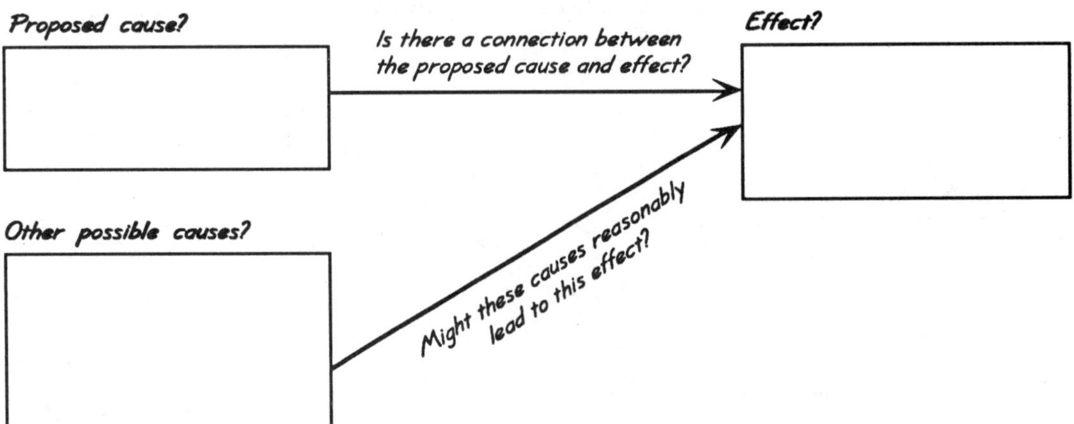

How strong is this argument? Why do you think so?

LESSON 5 Identifying and Evaluating Comparisons

Identifying Comparisons

Remember cue words for comparison reasoning, such as "like," "similar," "better," "worse," and so forth. Even without cue words, watch for items which compare two or more things. If you need help, refer to the section on **Comparisons** in the "Guide to Critical Thinking" (Unit 1).

Q Label each item below with the appropriate letter.

C The item involves **comparison** reasoning.

N The item does **not** involve comparison reasoning.

_______1. Willie took about two hours to build the model car.

_______2. This novel is 250 pages long.

_______3. Hans got to the general store before Lolita, so he must have driven his car.

_______4. The United States declared war on England in 1812 because of English violations of United States trade on the oceans and because of American desire to invade Canada.

_______5. In general, Native Americans had a healthier respect for land than did whites. Native Americans tended to use the land the way it was rather than changing it, for example by ploughing, to earn a living.

_______6. The power of tax is the power to destroy. So Maryland doesn't have the right to tax the United States Bank. (From *McCulloch v. Maryland* supreme court case)

_______7. The bank is necessary for the Congress to carry out its powers to tax and wage war.

[Continued on next page.]

[Continued from previous page.]

Evaluating Comparisons

> The key question for evaluating comparisons is
>
> How are the two cases similar and how are they different?
>
> In general, the more similarities, the better the comparison.

Use the key question for comparisons to evaluate each of the comparisons below.

8. The roses I fertilized are much larger than the other roses.

9. Since the federal government taxes state banks, state governments should be able to tax the federal bank. (An argument from *McCulloch v. Maryland* supreme court case.)

10. Since other countries in the early 1800s had tariffs (taxes on imported goods), the United States had to have tariffs also.

LESSON 6 How Did Early Industrialization Change Small New England Villages?

Although New England industrialization is best known for its large Waltham-style complexes, such as those at Lowell, Massachusetts, and Manchester, New Hampshire, it was in the villages and towns of New England that most of the early (1810–1860) industrialization took place. It took the form of one or two small textile factories appearing in the area. Few of these enterprises employed many workers, and individually they produced little cloth compared to the larger factories in the cities. But collectively these Rhode Island-style factories, as they were called, enjoyed greater employment and production than did their more well-known competitors. Most New England villagers continued to farm and make handicrafts, but the impact of industrial change was felt in everyday life.

In this lesson you are to analyze a pre-industrial New England town according to its social and economic characteristics. Then you are to make hypotheses about how this town might have changed socially and economically with industrialization.

Read the description below and answer the questions that follow.

Description of a New England Town, 1810

(Before any textile mills)

(1) Most people in this town in southern Massachusetts were farmers, but most farmers had to supplement their income by running grist or carding mills or doing other work. People in the towns regularly got together to help one family with a big task, such as a husking bee or a house raising. Wealthy farmers (those with perhaps $2,000 worth or property) were the highest class in town. They lived in substantial (larger, well constructed) homes with a few extra luxuries, such as imported wallpaper. Professionals, such as the lawyer and pastor (minister), were well respected, but the pastor did not make much money and had high expenses. Small farmers lived in modest homes with less land than the wealthier farmers, and landless people ranked below them. The town paid individuals to take care of outright paupers.

(2) Generally, adult males were jacks-of-all trades. They worked enough to provide for family needs, and sometimes to provide a few luxuries. Most products, such as food and clothing, were made in the households in town, not in factories. There was a significant amount of trading in town, but there was very little money. So trade was conducted by barter. Those products purchased at the town store were bought on credit and were paid in products or services. Credit accounts often lasted for years before they were paid off, and they sometimes lasted a lifetime.

(3) Centuries-old farming methods were used. Farmers didn't use much fertilizer, didn't rotate crops, and used traditional farm implements, such as the wooden plough. Almost all farm

[Continued on next page.]

[Continued from previous page.]

work was done by family members. Men and boys worked in the fields, women and girls cooked, did gardening, and spun yarn in the house. More prosperous farmers hired one or a few temporary workers during busy seasons or for big tasks. These workers lived with the farm family. Work was done based on daylight, the season, or until the task was completed.

(4) Non-farm enterprises consisted of handicraft, trading, and milling. All were done by individuals or small groups in addition to their regular farming, and most were not full-time or continuous. Each worker in these enterprises was skilled and did the whole job; for example, each cooper made the whole barrel.

(5) The population was very transient (temporary—moved around a lot). About half the household heads in 1810 had not been born in the town. Children were especially transient, because most had no land to inherit. Since many teenage children moved away from home, parental control over them was less than in previous generations.

Part I—Before Industrialization

Economic

1. How was trade conducted? Was money used?

2. How specialized was each worker?

3. What tools and methods were used to produce goods? (Old or new?)

4. Were most workers skilled or unskilled?

[Continued on next page.]

[Continued from previous page.]

5. Was farming or were other occupations dominant in the town?

Q Social

6. Did people cooperate or work individually?

7. How important was the family?

8. How stratified was this town?

9. What was the work environment, pace (how fast they worked), and schedule?

10. How important were luxury items/status symbols?

[Continued on next page.]

[Continued from previous page.]

Part II—Changes from Small Factories

Now suppose several small factories have moved into the town, employing 10–20% of the adult workers down to an age of about 14 years old. Each worker does one or two specific jobs, such as tending several power looms or carding machines. Workers are paid in cash at the mills. The mill owners will also need loans. Describe below how the town would change in each of the ways questioned in Part I.

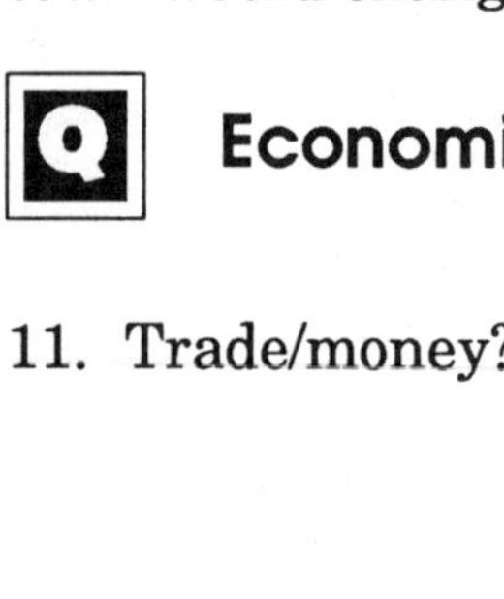

Economic

11. Trade/money?

12. Specialization?

13. Production methods?

14. Skilled/unskilled workers?

15. Farming dominant?

[Continued on next page.]

[Continued from previous page.]

Social

16. Cooperation vs. individuality?

17. Importance of the family?

18. Stratification?

19. Work environment (schedule and pace)?

20. Luxury items?

[Continued on next page.]

[Continued from previous page.]

Part III—A Farm Woman's Diary

As an elderly woman in the 1870s, Sarah Anna Emery recalled work and family life on the family farm in Newburyport, Massachusetts, where she grew up in the early nineteenth century. As a girl, knowing that she too would one day have household responsibilities, Sarah Anna was particularly watchful of her mother's activities.

Read this excerpt from Sarah Anna Emery's diary, and answer the questions that follow.

Sarah Anna Emery's Diary

From: *Reminiscences of a Nonagenarian*
by Sarah Anna Emery, 1879

(1) In those summer days, when my recollection first opens, Mother and Aunt Sarah rose in the early dawn, and taking the well-scoured wooden pails from the bench by the back door, repaired to the cow yard behind the barn. We owned six cows; my grandmother four. Having milked the ten cows, the milk was strained, the fires built, and breakfast prepared. Many families had milk for this meal, but we always had coffee or chocolate, with meat and potatoes. During breakfast the milk for the cheese was warming over the fire, in the large brass kettle. The milk being from the ten cows, my mother made cheese four days, Aunt Sarah having the milk the remainder of the week. In this way good-sized cheeses were obtained. The curd having been broken into the basket, the dishes were washed, and unless there was washing or other extra work, the house was righted. By the time this was done, the curd was ready for the press. Next came preparations for dinner, which was on the table punctually at twelve o'clock. In the hot weather we usually had boiled salted meat and vegetables, and, if it was baking day, a custard or pudding. If there was linen whitening on the grass, as was usual at this season, that must be sprinkled. After dinner the cheeses were turned and rubbed; then mother put me on a clean frock, and dressed herself for the afternoon. Our gowns and aprons, unless upon some special occasion, when calico was worn, were usually of blue-checked home-made gingham, starched and ironed to a nice gloss.

(2) In the sultry August afternoons, Mother and Aunt Sarah usually took their sewing to the cool back room, whose shaded door and windows overlooked the freshly-mown field, dotted by apple trees. Beyond the mossy stone wall stood the homestead of Uncle Samuel Thurlow (at that time this name was pronounced Thurrell), our next neighbor. Other buildings came to view, interspersed with hill and meadow, forest and orchards. The line of brown houses—very few were at that time painted—marked the position of the main road. Across rose the square meeting-house, crowning the high, precipitous hill upon which it was perched.

(3) My grandmother, after her afternoon nap, usually joined her daughters, with a pretence of knitting, but

[Continued on next page.]

Sarah Anna Emery's Diary

[Continued from previous page.]

she was not an industrious old lady. There was no necessity for work; and if idle hours are a sin, I fear the good woman had much to answer for. Leaning back in her easy-chair, she beguiled the time with watching the splendid prospect, with its ever-varying lights and shades, or joined in the harmless gossip of some neighboring woman, who had run in with her sewing, for an hour's chat.

(4) At five o'clock the men came from the field, and tea was served. The tea things washed, the vegetables were gathered for the morrow, the linen taken in, and other chores done. At sunset the cows came from the pasture. Milking finished, the milk strained, the day's labor was ended. The last load pitched on the hay mow, and the last hay cock turned up, my father and the hired man joined us in the cool back room, where bowls of bread and milk were ready for those who wished the refreshment. At nine o'clock, the house was still, the tired hands gladly resting from the day's toil.

21. List four ways the diary supports or weakens the hypotheses you listed in Part I about life in a New England village before mills started changing life significantly.

22. Evaluate the diary as a source of information.

[Continued on next page.]

[Continued from previous page.]

Part IV—The Davis Family, Mill Workers

Read the Davis family accounts that follow and answer the questions.

Davis Family Accounts

In September of 1803, William Davis married Rachel Humphry in Oxford, Massachusetts. By 1812 they had four children (they would eventually have seven children) and William Davis began to work for the newly organized Slater-Tiffany cotton mill. This document records the Davis family's work and obligations to the mill over a period of fifteen years.

1812—William and Rachel are living on their own farm in Oxford. William is working as a home weaver on an irregular basis. Their children are Jemima (age 9), John (age 6), Ebenezer (age 4), and Ruth (not yet 1 year).

February—The Davis family begins to purchase items at the store operated by the Slater-Tiffany cotton factory. Before William has done a day's work in the mill, he has built up a debt of $24.23 by various purchases:

1 box snuff

1 1/4 lbs. tobacco

1 lb. tea

4 1/2 lbs. brown sugar

3 qts. molasses

7 lbs. rice

2 1/2 qts. brandy

1 3/4 gal. gin

3 3/4 gal. rum

1 pt. size bottle

1 hair comb

September—William begins to pay the family debt and receives credit on his account by providing 168 feet of two-inch boards.

1813—William Davis begins to work in the cotton factory as a machine operator. His work is irregular, but throughout the year the family continues to make purchases at the mill store.

June—William Davis works 6 days

July—12 1/2 days

August—24 1/2 days

September—6 days

October—does not work

November—4 1/2 days

December—1 1/2 days

1814—January—William Davis gives a note to the Slater-Tiffany Mills, promising to pay the amount he owes to the mill store.

April—William Davis works 4 1/2 days in the mill. This is the only entry for William in the record books of the mill for this year.

December—Mary is born. She is William and Rachel's fifth child, the third girl.

1815—April—The William Davis family moves to a mill-owned tenement house. William Davis and the three oldest children are working in the mill: Jemima (now age 12), John (age 9), and Ebenezer (age 6 years, 11 months). They work regularly, from fifteen to twenty-two days a month for the remainder of the year.

[Continued on next page.]

Davis Family

[Continued from previous page.]

1816—In the first half of the year William, Jemima, John, and Ebenezer continue to work at the mill.

March—The Slater-Tiffany mill is employing about 101 workers.

July—Son Alonzo is born to William and Rachel. He is the sixth child and the third son. In July, the Slater-Tiffany mill has cut its work force to only 21 workers.

September—Slater-Tiffany has cut its work force to only 14; only William Davis continues to work in the mill.

1817—Jemima, John, and Ebenezer return to regular work in the mill, working 22 and 24 days per month in March.

June—Ruth Davis (now age 5 years and 6 months) begins work in the mill.

1818—William, Jemima, John, Ebenezer, and Ruth Davis continue to work regularly in the mill.

1819—The Davis family account in the records of the Slater-Tiffany Mill is closed.

1820—February—A seventh child, a boy named William, is born to William and Rachel Davis. Their family is now complete with 3 girls and 4 boys.

April—William and four of his children return to work in the mill. From the closing of the account book in June 1819 until April 1820, it is not clear whether or not the Davis family continued to live in the mill-owned tenement.

August—William Davis settles his accounts with the Slater-Tiffany company and the mill store. This is what he owed:

Amount carried over from
June and July $85.26

July 25 purchases .... .34

July 27 purchases .... .14

July 29 purchases .... .78

July 31 purchases .... .45

August 1 purchases .... .45

August 2 purchases .... .47

August 4 purchases .... .94

August 5 purchases 2.09

Total purchases July–August 5.66

For rent of tenement—April to July;
4 months at $25.00 per year $8.47

Total to date $99.39

This is what he earned:

for his work
in full to date inclusive (August 5, 1820) 97 days, 10 1/4 hours at $17 per month $64.04

for son John work
the same 16 weeks, 5 3/4 days at $1.25 per week $21.20

for son Ebenezer work
the same 16 weeks, 3 1/4 days at $1.00 per week $16.54

for daughter Jemima work
the same 17 weeks, 1 3/4 days at $2.00 per week $34.44

for daughter Ruth work
the same 15 weeks, 5 1/2 days at $.71 per week $11.27

Total $147.49

Amount due on account $99.39

Balance credited to William Davis in new account $48.10

[Continued on next page.]

Davis Family

[Continued from previous page.]

1821—October—Mary Davis begins work in the mill, age 6 years, 10 months.

1822—Jemima Davis is given a separate page in the mill account books and is charged separately for her room and board. She is now 19 years old.

1823—August—Ebenezer Davis leaves employment in the mill. He is now 17.

December—Alonzo Davis begins work in the mill, age 6 years, 7 months.

1825—April—John Davis, age 19, leaves employment in the mill.

1826—William, Ruth, Mary, and Alonzo continue to work in the mill. Jemima continues work in the mill and is listed separately in the account books.

1827—There is a change in the organization and management of the Slater-Tiffany Mills. The work force of 145 employees is reduced to 24. None of the Davis family members are listed. Elliot Mansfield, Jemima Davis' husband-to-be is listed among the new workers.

23. List four ways the accounts record confirms or weakens the hypotheses you listed in Part II about how mills changed life in a New England village.

24. Evaluate the Davis accounts as a source of information.

Handout: Economic and Sociological Concepts

Economic Terms

Barter: Trade without money; trading goods for goods.

Productivity: Amount of goods produced by each worker per hour. Productivity can be increased by using more advanced tools or machines, by organizing the work tasks more efficiently, or by other means.

Specialization: Each worker specializes in one job. As each person becomes more specialized he or she has a narrower range of skills so can do fewer jobs outside of the specialized job.

Skilled Workers: A job which requires particular skills requires skilled workers. Skilled workers have significant education or training to do the job. Unskilled jobs can be filled by a wide range of people without significant training.

Sociology Terms

Status: One's position or rank in society compared to others. People of high status have high prestige, or superior rank. Sometimes people buy objects, such as expensive luxuries, to show their status. These objects are called status symbols.

Social Class: A grouping of people according to social status, economic similarities (such as income level), or way of life.

Social Mobility: How easy it is to move up and down from one social class to another.

Stratification: The ranking of social classes from highest to lowest. More highly stratified societies have clearer divisions between classes, with less social mobility. A slave society is highly stratified since mobility out of the slave class is very difficult. Less stratified societies have more equality of wealth and prestige among its people and classes and have higher social mobility.

LESSON 7 What Were the Characteristics of the Ideal Woman in the Early 1800s?

Part I

Look at the pictures on the next two pages, then answer the following questions:

1. List as many characteristics of women in the early 1800s as you can.

2. Star the characteristics that are still true for women today.

[Continued on next page.]

[Continued from previous page.]

[Continued on next page.]

[Continued from previous page.]

MADAME DEAN'S SPINAL SUPPORTING CORSETS.

They support the Spine, relieve the muscles of the back, brace the shoulders in a natural and easy [illegible] graceful carriage to the wearer without discomfort, expanding the chest, thereby [illegible] full action to the lungs, and health and comfort to the body. Take the place of the ORDINARY [illegible] every respect, and are made of fine Coutil, in the best manner, in various styles and sold by agents [illegible] at popular prices. Mrs. Wm. Papes, Keota, Iowa, says:—I have been an invalid for six years [illegible] extensively for health, yet never received as much benefit as I have in a few weeks wear, of your [illegible] DEAN'S CORSET. I am gaining strength all the time, and could not do without it. It has proven to [illegible]

FREE our new book entitled: "Dress Reform for Ladies" with elegant wood engraving and Biography of Worth, the King of Fashion, Paris; also our New Illustrated Catalogue sent free to any address on [illegible] two 2-cent stamps to pay postage and packing.

AGENTS WANTED for these celebrated Corsets. No experience required. Four orders per day give the agent $150 monthly. Our agents report from four to twenty sales daily. $3.00 Outfit Free. Send for terms and full particulars. SCHIELE & CO., 390 Broadway, New York.

[Continued on next page.]

[Continued from previous page.]

3. How accurate are these pictures in showing women's actual roles and society's perceptions of women's roles? In other words, evaluate the pictures as sources, and evaluate their representativeness for generalizing about women in the early to mid-1800s.

4. Find at least one picture in a textbook, or other source, of a man or child from the early 1800s, and list the characteristics shown in the picture.

[Continued on next page.]

[Continued from previous page.]

Part II—The Cult of True Womanhood

In regard to women, the early 1800s has been labeled by some historians as "The Cult of True Womanhood." Each document which follows expresses a view of the ideal woman. Read the documents and then answer the questions.

Document A

The Young Lady's Book (New York; 1803), p. 28.
"It is, however, certain that in whatever situation of life a woman is placed from her cradle to her grave, a spirit of obedience and submission, pliability of temper, and humility of mind, are required from her."

Document B

George Burnap, *Sphere and Duties of Women* (5th ed., Baltimore, 1854), p. 47.
"She [woman] feels herself weak and timid. She needs a protector."

Document C

Mrs. John Sanford, *Woman in Her Social and Domestic Character* (Boston, 1842), p. 15.
"A really sensible woman feels her dependence. She does what she can, but she is conscious of inferiority, and therefore, grateful for support."

Document D

Eliza Farnham, *Woman and Her Era* (New York, 1864), p. 95.
"The purity of women is the everlasting barrier against which the tides of man's sensual nature surge."

Document E

Sara Jane Clarke, Letter "To an Unrecognized Poetess, June, 1846," *Greenwood Leaves* (2nd edition; Boston, 1850) p. 311.
"True feminine genius is ever timid, doubtful and clingingly dependent; a perpetual childhood."

[Continued on next page.]

[Continued from previous page.]

Document F

Mrs. John Sanford, *Woman*, p. 173.

"St. Paul knew what was best for women when he advised them to be domestic [stay at home]. There is composure at home; there is something sedative in the duties which home involves. It affords security not only from the world, but from delusions and errors of every kind."

Document G

Essay titles in women's magazines:

"Woman, Man's Best Friend," *The Young Ladies Oasis*, ed. N. L. Ferguson, (Lowell, 1851), p. 14.

"Woman, A Being to Come Home To," *Magnolia*, I, (1842), p. 4.

Document H

Samuel Jennings, "Proper Conduct of the Wife Toward Her Husband," from *The Married Lady's Companion or Poor Man's Friend*; 1808.

(1) "As it is your great wish to and interest, to enjoy much of your husband's company and conversation, it will be important to acquaint yourself with his temper, his inclination and his manner, that you may render your house, your person and your disposition quite agreeable to him.

(2) "Under the present circumstances, it is your interest to adapt yourself to your husband whatever his peculiarities. Again, nature has made him the stronger, the consent of mankind has given him superiority over his wife, his inclination is to claim his natural and acquired rights. He, of course, expects from you a degree of condescension for this makes him more sure of his natural claim.

(3) "In obedience then to this you ought to cultivate a cheerful and happy submission.

(4) "The great attentions practiced by most men in time of courtship are well calculated to raise in the female mind false expectations of a uniform continuance of the same officiousness after marriage. For the honeymoon you may not be disappointed. But afterwards, the charge of a family will teach any man he has more to do than carry on a courtship.

(5) "If any thoughts against this new behavior come to mind, check them. If indulged they will have a baneful effect on your temper and spread a gloom on your countenance so as to strip you of every charm.

(6) "If he does not come in the very hour or day that you expect him, instead of accusing him with neglect, be the considerate woman and take into view the various unavoidable delays with which he must meet in transacting business."

[Continued on next page.]

[Continued from previous page.]

Document I

Mrs. Sigourney, *Letters to Young Ladies*, p. 25.

"Needlework, in all its forms of use, elegance, and ornament, has been the appropriate occupation of women."

Document J

George Burnap, *Sphere* (1854), p. 64.

"[Marriage is] that sphere for which woman was originally intended, and to which she is so exactly fitted to adorn and bless, as the wife, the mistress of a home, the solace, the aid, and the counsellor of that one [her husband] for whose sake alone the world is of any consequence."

Document K

"Matrimony," *Lady's Amaranth*, II (Dec. 1839), p. 271.

"The man bears rule over his wife's person and conduct. She bears rule over his inclinations: he governs by law; she by persuasion....The empire of the woman is an empire of softness...her commands are caresses, her menaces are tears."

5. List the characteristics of the ideal woman as described in these documents.

6. To what extent are these characteristics still expected of women today?

[Continued on next page.]

[Continued from previous page.]

7. How reliable are these documents in telling us attitudes people held in the early 1800s about the ideal woman?

8. Evaluate this statement made by a historian. (That is, to what extent do you think it was true?)

   "Women in the mid-1800s were imprisoned by their own thinking in accepting the Cult of True Womanhood."

9. What information would help you better evaluate the statement in question 8?

LESSON 8 What Arguments Were Made for and against Women's Rights?

Part I—Seneca Falls

The documents which follow were shortened, portions being edited out. The documents were written and adopted at a convention held in Seneca Falls, New York, on July 19–20, 1848. The first is the Declaration of Sentiments; the second is a series of Resolutions taken by the convention. Read the two documents and answer the questions.

A. Declaration of Sentiments

We hold these rights to be self evident; that all men and women are created equal; that they are endowed by their Creator with certain inalienable rights; that among these are life, liberty, and the pursuit of happiness....

The history of mankind is a history of repeated injuries and seizures of power on the part of man toward woman, seeking to establish an absolute tyranny over her. To prove this, let facts be submitted to a candid world.

He has never permitted her to exercise her inalienable right to the elective franchise.

He has compelled her to submit to laws in the formation of which she has no voice.

He has withheld from her rights which are given to the most ignorant and degraded men—both natives and foreigners.

Having deprived her of this first right of a citizen, the elective franchise, thereby leaving her without representation in the halls of legislation, he has oppressed her on all sides.

He has made her, if married, in the eye of the law, civilly dead.

He has taken from her all right in property, even to the wages she earns.

...In the covenant of marriage, she is compelled to promise obedience to her husband, he becoming, to all intents and purposes, her master....

He has so framed the laws of divorce, as to what shall be the proper causes, and in case of separation, to whom the guardianship of the children shall be given, as to disregard the happiness of women....

He has monopolized nearly all the profitable employments, and from those she is permitted to follow, she receives but a scanty pay. He closes against her all the avenues to wealth and distinction which he considers most honorable to himself. As a teacher of theology, medicine, or law, she is not known.

He has denied her the facilities for obtaining a thorough education, all colleges being closed against her.

He has created a false public sentiment by giving to the world a different code of morals for men and women, by which moral delinquencies which exclude women from society are not only tolerated but deemed to be of little account to man.

[Continued on next page.]

Declaration of Sentiments

[Continued from previous page.]

He has endeavored, in every way that he could, to destroy her confidence in her own powers, to lessen her self-respect and to make her willing to lead a dependent and abject life.

Now...in view of the unjust laws above mentioned, and because women do feel themselves deprived of their most sacred rights, we insist that they have immediate admission to all rights and privileges which belong to them as citizens of the United States....

B. Resolutions at Seneca Falls

Resolved, That all laws which prevent woman from occupying such a station in society as her conscience shall dictate, or which place her in a position inferior to that of man, are contrary to the great precept of nature, and therefore of no force or authority.

Resolved, That woman is man's equal—was intended to be so by the Creator, and the highest good of the race demands that she should be recognized as such.

Resolved, That inasmuch as man, while claiming for himself intellectual superiority, does accord to woman moral superiority, it is preeminently his duty to encourage her to speak and teach, as she has an opportunity, in all religious assemblies.

Resolved, That the same amount of virtue, delicacy, and refinement of behavior that is required of woman in the social state, should also be required of man, and the same transgressions should be visited with equal severity on both man and woman.

Resolved, That it is the duty of the women of this country to secure to themselves their sacred right to the elective franchise [voting].

Part I—Declaration of Sentiments and Resolutions

1. Read the first and second paragraphs of the Declaration of Sentiments again. Why was it written this way?

[Continued on next page.]

[Continued from previous page.]

2. List the four most important grievances in this declaration.

3. How do you think most people would have reacted to these documents?

   Men:

   Women:

4. How would opponents of this view have argued against it?

5. What can you tell about the authors of these documents? (minimum of three things)

6. Should the Declaration of Sentiments be as famous as the Declaration of Independence? Explain your answer.

[Continued on next page.]

[Continued from previous page.]

7. Write a Declaration of Sentiments for women or men today of at least three paragraphs. Include at least three grievances women or men have today. (Use additional paper if necessary.)

[Continued on next page.]

[Continued from previous page.]

8. How many of the original grievances outlined in the Declaration of Sentiments still exist in some form today?

9. In 1852 the *New York Herald* ran an article on the women's conventions in which it asked, "Who are these women?" Its answer:

> Some of them are old maids, whose personal charms were never very attractive, and who have been sadly slighted by the masculine gender in general; some of them are women who have been badly mated...and they are therefore down upon the whole opposite sex; some, having so much of the virago [a strong, large, man-like woman] in their disposition, that nature appears to have made a mistake in their gender—mannish women, like hens that crow...there is [also] a class of wild enthusiasts and visionaries—very sincere but very mad....
>
> Of the male sex who attend these conventions for the purpose of taking part in them, the majority are hen-pecked husbands, and all of them ought to wear petticoats.

   Evaluate this argument.

10. Why do you think some people reacted this way?

[Continued on next page.]

[Continued from previous page.]

Part II—Woman Suffrage

One of the resolutions of the Seneca Falls Convention referred to the "sacred right to the elective franchise." The convention members wanted women to have the right to vote. In 1920 an amendment to the Constitution giving women the right to vote was ratified as the Nineteenth Amendment. The documents below consist of arguments made in the years prior to 1920. Some are arguments for and some are against woman suffrage.

Document A—Do a Majority of Women...Want the Ballot?

Statement of Mr. Franklin W. Collins of Nebraska before Senate Woman Suffrage Committee, April 1912

U.S., Congress, Senate, Committee on Woman Suffrage, 62nd Cong., 2d sess., Document no. 601, pp. 26–31.

Mr. Chairman and members of the honorable committee, I am opposed to the proposed amendment to the constitution granting the privileges and burdens of the franchise to women, and, with your indulgence, shall outline my objections to the same in a series of questions, intelligent and candid answers to which would seem to dispose of the plea which has been made for this so-called relief.

Why an amendment to the Constitution of the United States, and the preliminary steps leading thereto, when the States possess the power to extend the suffrage to women if they will?

Do a majority of the women of the United States want the ballot?

If not, and it is no where seriously contended that they do, should it be forced upon the majority by the minority?

Would it benefit womankind to have it?

Would it be wise to thrust the ballot upon those who do not seek it or want it?

Would it benefit the country?

Is it not incumbent upon its advocates to show that it would be beneficial to womankind or country, if not both?

Are there not too many stay-at-homes among the voters as it is?

After the novelty has worn away, and the privilege of voting becomes irksome, would not women be liable to stay at home in large and ever increasing numbers?

Is not this the experience of those States and communities where the experiment has been tried?

Is it not a fact that the persons we least like to see vote are the ones who invariably vote, and those we most desire to vote are the persons who often refrain from voting? Will this be changed when women secure the ballot?

Is not the influence of woman to-day greater without the ballot than it would or could be with it?

Is she not the life and hope of the home, the church, of charity work, and society, and are not her hands full to overflowing already?

In other words, is not the average good woman at the present time car-

[Continued on next page.]

Document A

[Continued from previous page.]

rying all the burdens which she has the time and strength to carry?

Can she add to her responsibilities without materially subtracting from her efficiency in the home, the church, and society?

Is not her influence as home-maker and a home-keeper far more helpful to humanity than it would be were she given the ballot, together with its accompaniments?

If, by her ballot, she should plunge the country into war, would she not be honor bound to fight by the side of man—to accept the consequences of her own exercise of political power?

Judged by its fruits, has the experiment of equal suffrage proven a success in Colorado, Wyoming, or elsewhere?

Have the women who would secure this privilege counted the cost of adding not alone the vote of the good and the cultured women to the electorate, but that of the illiterate, the ignorant, and the bad?

Show me the Congress or State legislature which would dare to overlook the wish and the will of womankind when once made known. Much has been said about the suffrage being a natural right, as, for instance, "Life, liberty, and the pursuit of happiness." Is suffrage such a right?

Is it not both a privilege and a burden imposed by the sovereignty which is the Government of the United States, under its Constitution, upon certain of the people of the country, who possess the qualifications fixed by that Constitution, and only upon those who measure up to such requirements?

If a natural or absolute right, to which all persons without regard to race or sex or color or what not are entitled to have and hold and exercise without question, why do we deprive our men of it until they arrive at the age of 21 years, why is it this so-called right is denied to the people of the Territories and the people of the District of Columbia?

If an absolute right, by what authority or color of authority does the State of Massachusetts, as well as other States, bar from the use and enjoyment of the suffrage men who do not possess certain prescribed educational qualifications?

Is it not true that every free lover, every socialist, every communist, and every anarchist the country over is openly in favor of female suffrage?

Does not the ballot in the hands of woman seem to give aid and comfort to schemes to overthrow the family and the private home?

Is not one of the saddest problems which the country faces to-day the disintegration of the American home?

Are not too many homes torn with discord and dissension, are not the divorce courts strewn with family skeletons, thick as leaves in the forests in Valambrosa?

Will the ballot in the hands of women pour oil on the troubled domestic waters?

Will not its inevitable tendency be to furnish still another cause of friction and irritation?

Speaking very seriously, and not wishing to be thought guilty of indelicacy, is it not a fact requiring no argument to support it that woman by her very

[Continued on next page.]

Document A

[Continued from previous page.]

organism and temperament—so fundamentally different and so delicate as compared with man—is not fitted to blaze man's trail or do man's work in the world any more than man is fitted to fill woman's sacred place and do her work in the world?

In other words, is not the so-called reform sought a reform against nature, unscientific and unsound?

Much has been said about the emancipation of woman, as if she were held in bondage through the tyranny of man or government. Are not the women of America the freest beings of their sex on the planet, and fully able to secure any of their sovereign rights, or redress any and all of their wrongs, if they will only unite and make their wants known—that is to say, if remedy by legislative action is possible?

There is a growing and a distinctly alarming tendency in this country on the part of women to escape the so-called drudgery of housekeeping, and particularly the burdens of child-bearing and child-rearing, so that we find many of those who are best equipped for wifehood and motherhood refusing to listen to its sacred call, while those who are illy equipped for it answering the same call unquestioningly.

Do you not think this movement has a strong tendency to encourage this exodus from "the land of bondage," otherwise known as matrimony and motherhood?

Is not the need of the land and the age to return to the old-fashioned, cardinal, and never-to-be-improved-upon virtues—a return to the first principles of right thinking and right living—a renaissance of the American family, which is fast being deserted by its former devotees; to speak plainly, that woman shall not flee from her high and holy mission as though it were a plague, so that no longer the finest product of America—the children—shall, in case they are permitted to arrive at all, be turned over to the tender mercies of hirelings for their training and mothering, or be allowed to bring themselves up with the chances that in the end away they will go to perdition, across lots; but instead of that they shall be trained in their own homes by their own mothers (I never knew a father who amounted to very much in this line, though he should boost all he can in the right direction); trained in the way they should go, in the full assurance of Holy Writ that when they are old they will not depart therefrom.

Finally, gentlemen, can the good women of the land help themselves, their country, or humanity, now or hereafter, in a more effective way than by the organization of a nationwide back-to-home movement?

Do not present propaganda and program mean a long step in the backward direction?

Is it not emphatically a movement away from home, away from nature, and away from those exalted ideals following which man and woman have struggled upward together from the depths of barbarism to the loftiest plane of civilization and progress the world has ever known?

I thank you.

[Continued on next page.]

[Continued from previous page.]

Document B—Some Reasons Why Women Oppose Votes for Women

Because the suffrage is not a question of right or of justice, but of what is best for the State; and if there is no question of right or of justice, there is no case for woman suffrage.

Because the demand for the ballot is made by a small minority of women and the majority of women depend upon men not to force it upon them.

Because the great advance of women in the last century—moral, intellectual, and economic—has been made without the vote, which goes to prove that the vote is not needed for their further advancement along the same lines.

Because women standing outside of politics, and therefore free to appeal to any party, are able to achieve reforms of greater benefit to the State than they could possibly achieve by working along partisan political lines.

Because the basis of government is physical force. It isn't law, but law enforcement, that protects society, and the physical power to enforce the law is neither possible nor desirable for women.

Vote no on Woman Suffrage Nov. 2

Woman Suffrage and Its Allies

Woman suffrage goes hand in hand with Feminism, Sex Antagonism and Socialism—doctrines which would abolish the marriage ceremony, strike a blow at the fundamentals of Christianity and revolutionize our social system.

If Suffragists deny this, ask them these questions:

Why is the National American Woman Suffrage Association publishing and selling the book entitled "The Case for Woman Suffrage"—a book filled with the most extreme feministic and socialistic arguments as reasons why women should vote?

Why has the National Woman Suffrage Association published and circulated "Bondwomen"—an infamous pamphlet attacking the marriage ceremony and characterizing wifehood as a species of slavery?

Why do suffrage organizations engage Charlotte Perkins Gilman, Winifred Harper Cooley, Rheta Childe Dehrr, Inez Milholand-Boisevain, Max Eastman and other radical feminists and socialists to speak and write for Woman Suffrage?

Why is every socialist and feminist an ardent woman suffragist?

Why has the New York Men's League for Woman Suffrage employed as its secretary Max Eastman, editor of "The Masses," a socialist publication, which printed the blasphemous poem, "God's Blunder?"

Why has no suffragist leader arisen to contradict the statement of Braverman, a socialist writer, that "No two social movements ever had so much in common as Woman Suffrage and Socialism?"

Why has no suffragist organization ever repudiated Socialism or Feminism, and why has no suffragist leader of any prominence ever written or spoken against those immoral propagandas?

No one can afford to be neutral regarding Socialism or Feminism, and no one can do anything, directly or indirectly, to advance those movements without helping to lay the axe at the tap-root of Christian civilization.

[Continued on next page.]

[Continued from previous page.]

Document C

The Ohio Ass'n Opposed to Woman's Suffrage, Chamber of Commerce Building, Columbus, Ohio

Voters.

In our campaign before the voters of the State, we rest our cause on these fundamental truths:

First—The Majority of women do not want the vote.

According to the public statement of the Ohio Suffrage Association its membership is 32,000, or less than 3 per cent of the women of the State over 21 years of age.

It is unwise, unfair and unjust to force upon a majority of women, a measure which is obnoxious to all their ideals of womanhood.

Second—There is no evidence in the states where women vote that they have contributed anything to the general welfare which has not been duplicated in other states where female franchise does not exist.

All necessary and permanent moral and social reform must be rooted in the home life of the people. It is in the retirement of this quiet home life and not in the publicity of a noisy political campaign that true womanhood seeks an opportunity to serve the state.

Third—The payment of taxes and the right to vote have no connection whatever.

A man may own property in half a dozen places in the State, and in other states, but he can vote in only one place—the place of his residence. Minors are fully taxed on their property and so are aliens, but neither class can vote.

Fourth—Women lack the physical ability to exercise the franchise on the same terms as men.

Women are now exempt from jury service and liabilities to police service, including a call to arms in defense of the country.

This exemption far more than compensates any gain which even the most ardent suffragists claim would result from conferring the right of suffrage upon women.

Fifth—It is a mistake to presume that all women will vote right on moral issues. Experience proves that many of the worst ills of social life are due to the influence of women of low ideals of right and wrong, or of degrading morals. Women of this type would be a most dangerous element in political life and would lend themselves to the support of immoral issues, backed by designing demagogues in a manner which could not be counteracted by women of reputation and character.

To the ever increasing courtesy of men as shown in the social relation of life as well as to their constant protection in business affairs, women owe a debt of gratitude. In view of this courtesy and protection, the demand for so-called "Women's Rights" is both unbecoming and ungenerous.

Vote no on Amendment No. 23

Further literature upon request.

[Continued on next page.]

[Continued from previous page.]

Document D

Grace Duffield Goodwin, *The Westfield Leader*, Wednesday, February 18, 1914. Issued by the Plainfield Branch N. J. Assn. Opposed to Woman Suffrage

Theory vs. Fact

The suffragists are urging an amendment to the Federal Constitution by which all the States shall speedily enfranchise their women. These women are citizens now in the eyes of the law; no ballot will make them more so. They are entitled to the same protection of life, property and civil rights, which is accorded to men, and in many instances they are given more than their share of all these things.

They are at present exempt from political burdens and responsibilities, free from political intrigues and alliances, in demand in all States as intelligent non-partisan servants of the common weal. They are kept out of no occupation or profession; they have every educational advantage; they have in this State and in many others no disabilities under the law. The effort to represent them as oppressed, enslaved, suffering under grave legal and economic injustice is futile, because such a statement is disproved in the making. The generous endeavors of men have produced within the last ten years a body of protective legislation for woman in industry which puts her in a privileged class under the law. The Maternity Law of Massachusetts, New Hampshire, Connecticut and New York is a case in point. The men did this.

We do not need women to "mother" the government. We do not need to see the "mother spirit" in the Supreme Court. We need mothers where mothering counts—in personal contact with the lives of individual children. This is being made a matter of legislation when it should be parental control and parental love. We need better fathers and mothers, better homes, the family still the social unit with a common interest and sympathy. We do not need more women politicians, more women office seekers, more women street orators—which types are appearing in this suffrage agitation far too frequently for safety.

The theory that conditions will be bettered by the entrance for women into political life is disproved by the facts. The theories of injustice, oppression, etc., are refuted by the facts. The government's need of such help is not apparent; a woman's power to render any better service than a man is not apparent. Women's unrest, discontent, confused thinking, selfish individualism are everywhere in evidence in an agitation which has no claim to the attention of those who want the best for the country and the best for its womanhood.

The country does not need it.

The women as a whole do not want it.

The conditions do not warrant it.

Comparisons are not favorable to it.

Our present governmental system makes for general justice. Only 10% of the women are taxpayers, and in several States they have "taxpaying

[Continued on next page.]

Document D

[Continued from previous page.]

suffrage"—which they do not use. Property is not the basis of the American ballot. The statement that "one half of the country is governed without its consent" is fallacious. The women as a whole appear to agree that the present system of government is well adapted to our needs and circumstances. The government has the consent of its governed, except that minority of women who are apparently neither students of history, political science nor logic, therefore who are better off to be governed than to be governors.

Document E—Eminent Catholic Prelates Oppose Woman Suffrage

The Voice of Common Sense

From the Catholic Encyclopedia, vol. 15, p. 694, published in 1912 under the imprimatur of Archbishop (now Cardinal) Farley of New York.

"The indirect influence of women which in a well-ordered state makes for the moral order, would suffer severe injury by political equality. The opposition expressed by many women to the introduction of woman suffrage as for instance, the New York Association Opposed to Woman Suffrage, should be regarded by Catholics as, at least, the voice of common sense."

James Cardinal Gibbons.

From a letter to Mrs. Robert Garrett of Baltimore, April 22, 1913.

Equal rights do not imply that both sexes should engage promiscuously in the same pursuits, but that each should discharge those duties which are adapted to its physical constitution. The insistence on a right of participation in active political life is undoubtedly calculated to rob woman of all that is amiable and gentle, tender and attractive; to rob her of her innate grace of character and give her nothing in return but masculine boldness and effrontery. When I deprecate female suffrage, I am pleading for the dignity of woman, I am contending for her honor, I am striving to perpetuate those peerless prerogatives inherent in her sex, those charms and graces which exalt womankind and make her the ornament and coveted companion of man. Woman is queen indeed, but her empire is the domestic kingdom. The greatest political triumphs she would achieve in public life fade into insignificance compared with the serene glory which radiates from the domestic shrine, and which she illuminates and warms by her conjugal and motherly virtues. If she is ambitious of the dual empire of public and private life, then like the fabled dog beholding his image in the water she will lose both, she will fall from the lofty pedestal where nature and Christianity have placed her and will fail to grasp the scepter of political authority from the strong hand of her male competitor.

[Continued on next page.]

Document E

[Continued from previous page.]

Cardinal Farley

(From a newspaper interview in Los Angeles.)

I do not believe in woman suffrage. I think it best for all women to leave to man politics, and, as far as possible, the affairs of government. It is my belief that women will soon tire of the ballot in states in which they have secured it. A fad, I do not believe it will last.

The Rt. Rev. John S. Foley, Bishop of Detroit

The political arena is not the place for the highest development of all that is best in woman. Nothing but degradation can come from placing gentle women in the voting places to come in contact with all sorts and conditions of men. No good can be accomplished by merely placing the ballot in the hands of women, and the evils which will certainly result will make every husband and father who has respect for the women of his family regret that woman suffrage was ever adopted.

Archbishop Messmer of Milwaukee

(From an address on "Woman's Rights.")

The theory that demands equal rights between the sexes must be denied absolutely. It is a mistake to say equal rights instead if similar rights, for women have certain rights that men have not, and men have certain rights that women have not. In regard to politics, why should woman have equal rights? Politics means the ruling of nations, and no one who understands this would demand equal rights. Equal rights would interfere with woman's calling. It would destroy her influence on mankind. The modern women's question is the outcome of the French Revolution.

Archbishop Moeller of Cincinnati

(From a letter to the clergy of his diocese.)

It is a movement that does not appeal to us, because we feel that it will bring women into a sphere of activities that is not in accord with their retiring modesty, maidenly dignity and refinement. We fear that suffrage women will cease to be the queens of the home. Let the women devote themselves, as far as their duties permit, to works of charity for which nature has so well fitted them. It not infrequently happens that owing to apathy and indifference, measures have been carried that have not the proper endorsement. We request the women not to fail to sign the anti-suffrage list if they do not wish to, or do not believe that they should, enroll themselves under the banner of the suffragists. Pastors might urge the women from the pulpit to declare themselves in regard to this matter when the opportunity presents itself.

Issued for Massachusetts Anti-Suffrage Committee

[Continued on next page.]

[Continued from previous page.]

Document F

Issued by The Wage Earners' Anti-Suffrage League

Wage Earning Women

Stop—Think—Reason

Can the workingman use his vote to get work? No.

Thousands of voters are out or work in this country to-day.

Can the working man use his vote to raise wages? No.

The ballot has no relation to man and his work.

Why should the vote do for you what it has failed to do for men?

What must a woman do to obtain work and raise her wages?

She must apply herself—application develops efficiency; efficiency develops success.

Ask those who have succeeded.

Do not believe those who have failed.

* * *

Wage Earning Women

Stop! Think! Reason!

Can the workingman use his vote to get work? No.

Thousands of voters are out of work in this country to-day.

Can the workingman use his vote to raise his wages? No.

The ballot has no relation to man and his wages. Neither would it have any relation to woman and her wages.

Votes cannot make work when there is no work.

Votes cannot increase wages when there is no natural increase in business.

Document G—Quotations from the Opinions of Authorities on the Subject of Woman Suffrage

Former Attorney General George W. Wickersham:

"The real significance of the ballot as not being a detached privilege in itself, but as indicative of full citizenship, implies obligations of various kinds, such as service on juries, willingness to perform military service when required, etc. In my opinion, the effect of injecting women into politics is bound to be injurious upon society as a whole and to result in the destruction of the family organization as it has been known in the past. At present a great many women are inclined to regard the subject as involving merely the dropping of a ballot in the box taking a short time, but, as a matter of fact, a woman cannot fitly discharge all those duties of citizenship unless she gives to them an amount of time inconsistent with the performance of her home duties. This aspect of it is particularly acute in large cities."

[Continued on next page.]

Document G

[Continued from previous page.]

Richard H. Dana:

"The truth is, the ballot for women is not needed—and if they were ever called upon to combine and work in antagonism to the men, which they must do if their vote is really needed, the evils of the conflict would strike at the very foundations of our social system."

Hon. Thos. F. Bayard:

"There never was a falser statement than that the women of America need any greater protection further than the love borne to them by their fellow countrymen. Do not imperil the advantages which they have or interfere with relations which are founded upon the laws of nature herself."

Hon. Stanley Bowdle of Ohio, Member of Congress:

"No, we cannot have the millennium by law, and women will learn this, as men have been compelled to learn it. If we could, this nation would long since have been the scene of millennial glory surpassing anything dreamed of by the prophets of Israel, for we certainly have the laws."

Melinda Scott, President of the Trade Unionists:

"We are skeptical—we cannot see that Suffrage will mean all to us that Suffragists purpose."

Right Rev. Daniel Sylvester Tuttle, Presiding Episcopal Bishop of the United States:

"It is not fair to women to give them the ballot. Already women are doing more than half the world's work. It is said that suffrage would eliminate many of the social evils. That remains to be seen. Many of the women who would vote are degraded women, who could be influenced by prejudice and money, and it seems to me there would be merely an addition to the corrupt vote."

Dr. S. Wier Mitchell:

"The best of the highest evolution of mind will never be safely reached until woman accepts the irrevocable decree which made her woman and not man. Something in between she cannot be."

Document H

From: *Political Equality*, leaflet published by the National American Woman Suffrage Association. (after 1900)
(Pamphlet distributed to women.)

Women In the Home
by Susan W. Fitzgerald

We are forever being told that the place of woman is in the home. Well, so be it. But what do we expect of her in the home? Merely to stay in the home is not enough. She is a failure unless she does certain things for the home. She must make the home min-

[Continued on next page.]

Document H

[Continued from previous page.]

ister, as far as her means allow, to the health and welfare, moral as well as physical, of her family, and especially her children. She, more than anyone else, is held responsible for what they become.

She is responsible for the cleanliness of her house.

She is responsible for the wholesomeness of the food.

She is responsible for the children's health.

She, above all, is responsible for their morals, for their sense of truth, of honesty and of decency, for what they turn out to be.

How far can the mother control these things? She can clean her own rooms, but if the neighbors are allowed to live in filth, she cannot keep her rooms from being filled with bad airs and smells, or from being infested by vermin.

She can cook her food well, but if dealers are permitted to sell poor food, unclean milk or stale eggs, she cannot make the food wholesome for her children.

She can care for her own plumbing and refuse, but if the plumbing in the rest of the house is unsanitary, if garbage accumulates and the halls and stairs are left dirty, she cannot protect her children from the sickness and infection that these conditions bring.

She can take every care to avoid fire, but if the house has been badly built, if the fire-escapes are insufficient or not fire-proof, she cannot guard her children from the horrors of being maimed or killed by fire.

She can open her windows to give her children the air that we are told is so necessary, but if the air is laden with infection, with tuberculosis and other contagious diseases, she cannot protect her children from this danger.

She can send her children out for air and exercise, but if the conditions that surround them on the streets are immoral and degrading, she cannot protect them from these dangers.

Alone, she cannot make these things right. Who or what can? The city can do it, the city government that is elected by the people, to take care of the interests of the people.

And who decides what the city government shall do?

First, the officials of that government; and, second, those who elect them.

Do the women elect them? No, the men do. So it is the men and not the women that are really responsible for the unclean houses, unwholesome food, bad plumbing, danger of fire, risk of tuberculosis and other diseases, immoral influences of the street. In fact, men are responsible for the conditions under which the children live, but we hold women responsible for the results of those conditions. If we hold women responsible for the results, must we not, in simple justice, let them have something to say as to what these conditions shall be? There is one simple way of doing this. Give them the same means that men have, let them vote.

Women are by nature and training, housekeepers, let them have a hand in the city's housekeeping, even if they introduce an occasional housecleaning.

[Continued on next page.]

[Continued from previous page.]

Document I

From: U.S., Congress, Senate, Joint Committee, 62nd Cong., 2nd sess., S. Document 601, pp. 16–20. Statements by Caroline Lowe and Leonora O'Reilly to the Joint Judiciary Committee and Woman Suffrage Committee of the Senate, April 23, 1912.

Statement of Miss Caroline A. Lowe, of Kansas City, Mo.

Gentleman of the committee, it is as a wage earner and on behalf of the 7,000,000 wage-earning women in the United States that I wish to speak.

I entered the ranks of the wage earners when 18 years of age. Since then I have earned every cent of the cost of my own maintenance, and for several years was a potent factor in the support of my widowed mother.

Need of the Ballot. The need of the ballot for the wage-earning women is a vital one. No plea can be made that we have the protection of the home or are represented by our fathers or brothers. We need the ballot that we may broaden our horizon and assume our share in the solution of the problems that seriously affect our daily lives. There is no question that the exercise of the right to vote on matters of public concern enlarges the sense of public responsibility. While in Colorado, visiting a friend who had formerly been a teacher in Kansas, she assured me that the average woman teacher in Colorado, where the women have the full right of franchise, is as fully informed on all political matters as is the average man teacher in Kansas, while the average woman teacher in Kansas ranks below the man in this respect.

We need the ballot for the purpose of self-protection. Last Saturday afternoon, at the closing hour at Marshall Field's in Chicago, a young woman cashier fell on the floor in a dead faint and was carried away by her fellow workers. Long hours of the rush and strain of the Saturday shopping had overcome her. The 10-hour law in not a 10-hour law for us. We must be up at 6 in order to be at work by 8. It requires two hours after work for us to reach home and eat our evening meal. Fourteen hours out of the twenty-four are consumed entirely by our daily efforts to make a living. If we secure any education or amusement it leaves us but seven or eight hours for sleep, and this generally in unsanitary and unwholesome surroundings.

Does the young woman clerk in Marshall Field's need any voice in making the law that sets the hours of labor that shall constitute a day's work?

Has the young woman whose scalp was torn from her head at the Lawrence mill any need of a law demanding that safety appliances be placed upon all dangerous machinery?

The Working Woman and the Workingman. From the standpoint of wages received we wage earners know it to be almost universal that the men in the industries receive twice the wage granted to us, although we may be doing the same work and should have the same pay. We women work side by side with our brothers. We are children of the same parents, reared in the same homes, educated in the same schools, ride to and fro on the same early morning and late

[Continued on next page.]

Document I

[Continued from previous page.]

evening cars, work together the same number of hours in the same shops, and we have equal need of food, clothing, and shelter. But at 21 years of age our brothers are given a powerful weapon for self-defense, a larger means for growth and self-expression.

We working women, even because we are women and find our sex not a source of strength, but a source of weakness and offering a greater opportunity for exploitation, are denied this weapon.

Gentlemen of the committee, is there any justice underlying such a condition? If our brother workingmen are granted the ballot with which to protect themselves, do you not think that the working women should be granted this same right?

Discrimination Against Disfranchised Class. You say the ballot is not a factor as a means of discrimination between the workingman and the working woman. We found the most striking example of the falsity of this statement a few years ago in Chicago. The Chicago teachers (mostly women), firemen, and policemen had had their salaries cut because of the poverty of the city. The teachers' salaries were cut the third time. They organized to investigate the reason for the reduction. Margaret Haley was selected to carry on the investigation. As a result, she unearthed large corporations that were not paying the legal amount of taxes. The teachers forced the issue, and as a result nearly $600,000 in taxes was annually forced from the corporations and turned into the public treasury. What was done with it? The policemen and firemen had the cut in their salaries restored, while the teachers did not. Instead, the finance committee recommended and the board of education appropriated the teachers' share to pay coal bills, repairs, etc. Why was this? It was a clear case of the usual treatment accorded to a disfranchised class.

Industrial Revolution Precedes Political Evolution. However, Mr. Chairman, as students of sociology we are forced to recognize the fact that the ballot has never yet been granted by a ruling class because of the needs of a serving class.

Almost without exception the extension of the franchise has taken place only when the needs of the industrial development have demanded a larger degree of freedom upon the part of the serving class, so that the serving class, driven by the very pressure of economic need, has organized as a class, and, after a struggle, has wrested from the grasp of the ruling class a larger share in the powers of government.

If to-day, taking your places as men of affairs in the world's progress, you step out in unison with the eternal upward trend toward true democracy, you will support the suffrage amendment now before the committee. [Continued applause.]

Statement of Miss Leonora O'Reilly, of New York City.

Mr. Chairman and gentlemen of the committee: Yes; I have outdone the lady who went to work at 18 by five years. I have been a wage earner since I was a little over 13. I, too,

[Continued on next page.]

Document I

[Continued from previous page.]

know whereof I speak; that is the reason I do not want to play a bluff game with you any longer. You can not or will not make laws for us; we must make laws for ourselves. We working women need the ballot for self-protection; that is all there is to it. We have got to have it.

We work long, long hours and we do not get half enough to live on. We have got to keep decent, and if we go "the easy way" you men make the laws that will let you go free and send us into the gutter. [Applause.]

We have gone before legislature after legislature making our pleas for justice. We have seen the game as you play it. What is it? We go there and we are told the same old tommyrot—let men do this for you. I tell you as a bit of business experience if you let anybody do a thing for you they will do you. That is business. [Applause.]

We are not getting a square deal; we go before legislature after legislature to tell our story, but they fail to help the women who are being speeded so high in the mills and in factories, from 54 to 72 hours in stores in New York, and 92 hours in one week in subcellar laundries. Who cares? Nobody! Nobody does; nobody cares about making laws so long as we get cheap and nasty things in the market. Working women come before you and tell you these things and think you will do something for them. Every man listening is convinced that the girls are telling the truth. It is only when you think of them as your own girls that you have the right to make laws for them. Every man listening wants to do the fair thing, but just as soon as our backs our turned, up comes the representative of the big interest and says, "Lad, you are dead politically if you do what those women ask." They know it is true, and we get nothing, because all the votes are owned.

Every vote you cast is owned, and it is the owned vote which has fought our women. Go before legislatures as you will, the only argument that you can bring in to the man in politics—he is there to go up the ladder, decently if he can, but he will go up anyhow, if he can—the only argument that you can bring to that man is the power of the ballot. When we can say to him. "Man do this and we will return you so many million votes," he will listen and act.

We working women want the ballot, not as a privilege but as a right. You say you have only given the ballot as an expediency; you have never given it as a right; then we demand it as an expediency for the 8,000,000 working women. All other women ought to have it, but we working women must have it. [Applause.]

[Continued on next page.]

[Continued from previous page.]

Document J

Remarks by Mrs. Zerelda G. Wallace, of Indiana to Senate Judiciary Committee, January 1880 From: U.S., Congress, Senate, Judiciary Committee, *Appendix to the Report on Suffrage*, 49th Cong., 1st Sess., S. Rept. 70, pp. 21–22.

Mr. Chairman and gentlemen of the committee: It is scarcely necessary to recite that there is not an effect without a cause. Therefore it would be well for the statesmen of this nation to ask themselves the question, What has brought women from all parts of this nation to the capital at this time? What has been the strong motive that has taken us away from the quiet and comfort of our own homes and brought us before you to-day?

A short time ago I went before the legislature of Indiana with a petition signed by 25,000 women, the best women in the State. I appeal to the memory of Judge McDonald to substantiate the truth of what I say. Judge McDonald knows that I am a home-loving, law-abiding, tax-paying woman of Indiana, and have been for fifty years. When I went before our legislature and found that one hundred of the vilest men in our State, merely by possession of the ballot, had more influence with the law-makers of our land than the wives and mothers of the nation, it was a revelation that was perfectly startling.

You must admit that in popular government the ballot is the most potent means of all moral and social reforms. As members of society, as those who are deeply interested in the promotion of good morals, of virtue, and of the proper protection of men from the consequences of their own vices, and of the protection of women, too, we are deeply interested in all the social problems with which you grappled so long unsuccessfully. We do not intend to depreciate your efforts, but you have attempted to do an impossible thing. You have attempted to represent the whole by one-half; and we come to you to-day for a recognition of the fact that humanity is not a unit; that it is a unity; and because we are one-half that go to make up that grand unity we come before you to-day and ask you to recognize our rights as citizens of this Republic.

I say to you, then, we come as one-half of the great whole. There is an essential difference in the sexes. Mr. Parkman labored very hard to prove what no one would deny, that there is an essential difference in the sexes, and it is because of that very differentiation, the union of which in home, the recognition of which in the church brings the greatest power and influence for good, and the recognition of which in the Government would enable us finally, as near as it is possible for humanity, to perfect our form of government. Probably we can never have a perfect form of government, but the nearer we approximate to the divine the nearer will we attain to perfection; and the divine government recognizes neither caste, class, sex, nor nationality. The nearer we approach to that divine ideal the nearer we will come to realizing our hopes of finally securing at least the most perfect form of human government that it is possible for us to secure.

[Continued on next page.]

[Continued from previous page.]

Part II—Woman Suffrage

11. On a separate piece of paper, write at least five arguments for or against woman suffrage. Use arguments taken from the documents (write the document letter next to each argument), and add some of your own if you'd like.

12. Evaluate the arguments made by Franklin Collins in Document A.

13. Evaluate one argument made in Document B.

14. What assumption do the Catholic clergymen make in Document E?

[Continued on next page.]

[Continued from previous page.]

15. To what groups were the antisuffragists appealing?

16. To what group was the suffragist Susan Fitzgerald appealing in Document H?

17. Evaluate an argument made in Document I.

18. Evaluate an argument made in Document J.

Should Women Have the Right to Vote?

Read Documents A–J in this lesson (pp. 53–67) and fill in this chart. Use the back if you need more space. After completing the chart, write your view on whether women should have the right to vote on the back or on a separate piece of paper.

Document	2 or 3 Key Arguments	Evaluate 1 Argument
A Franklin Collins		
B Antisuffrage Leaflets		
C Ohio Association Opposed to Woman's Suffrage		
D Plainfield Branch N. J. Assn. Opposed to Woman Suffrage		
E Eminent Catholic Prelates		
F Wage Earners' Anti-Suffrage League		
G Quotations by Authorities		
H Susan Fitzgerald		
I Caroline Lowe and Leonora O'Reilly		
J Mrs. Zerelda Wallace		

LESSON 9 Was Andrew Jackson a Representative of the Common People?

Andrew Jackson was elected president in 1828. This lesson presents two interpretations on the issue of whether Jackson was a representative of the common people against the rich. Read the interpretations and answer the questions which follow.

Historian A

(1) When Andrew Jackson was elected President in 1828, he symbolized the change in politics from control by the rich aristocrats to control by the common people. The rich had built a system based on an alliance of government and business. This alliance was pushed for or adopted in such policies as the U.S. Bank and the American System [tariffs and government-supported transportation to help business]. In the 1820s the common people became increasingly discontented with the Neofederalist program, however. Western farmers blamed the Panic of 1819 on the tight money policies of the U.S. Bank. Workingmen were also upset by rising prices, which they associated with the U.S. Bank, and by the loss of control and craftsmanship which they experienced in the spreading factory system.

(2) More of the common people could vote in the 1820s, and this allowed them to elect a president who would represent their interests—Andrew Jackson. The new president began immediately to make changes by replacing government officials with representatives of the common people. He brought in reformers as unofficial advisors, called the kitchen cabinet. These advisors would help bring about the necessary changes in the rich-dominated system.

(3) One of the symbols of privilege and dominance by the rich was the U.S. Bank. Under the direction of Nicholas Biddle, the Bank had extensive control over the monetary system (such as prices and credit) of the country. President Jackson believed that true democracy included equality of economic opportunity as well as political equality. So, Jackson attacked the Bank. An examination of Jackson's veto message of the Bank recharter shows not a criticism of the Bank in terms of too much inflation or not enough money expansion. Rather, it shows a criticism that the Bank had too much power and gave extensive privileges to the rich. Jackson characterized the Bank War as a contest between the *rich and powerful* and the *humble members of society*.

(4) Jackson was extremely popular with the common man after he defeated the U.S. Bank. The rich conservatives were depressed by Jackson's reforms. They banded together into the Whig Party in order to defeat their new opponent whom they called *King Andrew the First*. Eventually, the Whigs adopted mass rallies and empty slogans to attract popular support at election time. They avoided talking about the issues which Jackson brought to the nation's attention.

[Continued on next page.]

Historian A

[Continued from previous page.]

(5) As a result, the Whigs regained control of the government in 1840. Conservative policies were reimposed on the country. However, the rich conservatives could not undo most of Jackson's reforms. Jackson had established the principles that the lower classes were to have more say in the political decisions of the nation, and that the government would play a strong role in the economic system. These principles became the liberal tradition which was reinforced by the other liberal presidents: Theodore Roosevelt, Woodrow Wilson, and Franklin Roosevelt. The rich conservatives criticized the liberal policies as too radical. However, the result of liberal reform was to keep the capitalists from destroying capitalism.

Historian B

(1) Liberal historians, such as Historian A, have characterized the Jacksonian period of American History as a struggle between the liberal viewpoints of the working class, led by the Democratic Party of Andrew Jackson, and the conservative viewpoints of the wealthy class, led by the Whigs. This narrow characterization oversimplifies and distorts a much more complex struggle in the 1820s and 1830s.

(2) First of all, Jackson himself was not a common man, but rather an aristocrat in Tennessee. Likewise, many of the leading Jacksonians were men of great wealth or men eager to become wealthy. They took political positions to gain the support of workers, but used it to help aspiring capitalists, not workingmen.

(3) There were, in fact, rich and poor in both the Democratic and Whig Parties. The whole idea that there was a struggle of the poor (organized in one party) against the rich (united in the other party) is mistaken. This is shown in an examination of the two parties in New York State. Both parties included big and small businessmen, farmers, workers, and used the same slogans and appeals.[1]

(4) Through studying voting patterns one is led to the conclusion that ethnic and religious differences, rather than class difference, are what influenced people to vote for one party over the other. There really were no significant differences between the Democrats and the Whigs in terms of political-economic ideology (beliefs). Americans were simply too individualistic to be organized by classes into political parties. Almost all Americans believed in liberal ideals such as equality of opportunity. Both parties appealed broadly to these ideals and avoided touchy issues.

(5) What the liberal historians have described as a struggle between the parties of the rich and poor was, in

[Continued on next page.]

Historian B

[Continued from previous page.]

reality, a consensus [agreement] of political beliefs by both parties. Americans in the Jacksonian period differed in their viewpoints not because of class differences, but rather because of ethnic and religious differences. Andrew Jackson, far from being the champion of farmers and workers, was an astute politician who used class rhetoric to gain support for his own political ends.

Endnote for Historian B

1. From Lee Benson, *The Concept of Jacksonian Democracy: New York as a Test Case*, Princeton University Press, 1961, pp. 148–50, pp. 183–85. This information was summarized by Historian B.

   In a study of voting patterns in counties in New York State in the 1844 Election two results were noted:

   First, within the same county there was no significant relationship between the wealth of towns and how those towns voted in the 1844 Election. That is, some wealthy towns voted overwhelmingly Democrat while other wealthy towns voted overwhelmingly against the Democrats. Likewise, some poor towns voted Democrat while others did not.

   For example, in Delaware County two towns (Davenport and Hamden) of about equal economic status (average value of dwelling per family was $305 for Davenport and $502 for Hamden) had completely different voting percentages for the Democrats. Davenport gave the Democrats 81.1 percent of its vote, and Hamden gave 31.8 percent. One of the wealthiest towns (Franklin) gave the Democrats only 44.9 percent of its vote. The richest town in the county (Delhi) and one of the poorest towns (Masonville) gave the Democrats about the same percentage of votes (48.5 and 46.8 percent, respectively).

   This pattern is the same for all the other counties studies in New York State. Urban areas were not studied since the average value of dwelling per family could not be constructed from the available information.

   Second, ethnic group and religious affiliation were very much related to how people voted. We can only estimate group percentages, but the estimates clearly show the basic point that ethnic group and religious group were important. In the 1844 Election Yankees were fairly evenly divided between Whigs (55 percent) and Democrats (45 percent), Negroes voted about 95 percent for the Whigs. Catholic immigrants (Irish French and French Canadians) voted overwhelmingly Democrat (80 percent to 95 percent) while Protestant immigrants (Irish, Welsh, Scots, and English) voted overwhelmingly Whig (75 percent to 90 percent). It is interesting to note the difference between Catholic and Protestant Irish voting.

   These estimates were made by comparing the vote in the counties and towns in the 1844 Election with the ethnic and religious make-up of those counties and towns. The estimates lead to the conclusion that the native Americans were rather evenly divided between the two parties while the immigrant groups leaned strongly for one party or the other.

[Continued on next page.]

[Continued from previous page.]

Q Historian A

1. What is the main point of Historian A's interpretation?

2. Evaluate the reasoning used in the first paragraph, second sentence.

3. Evaluate the reasoning used in the last two sentences of paragraph four and the first sentence of paragraph five.

4. Evaluate one piece of evidence used to support this interpretation.

5. What is the author's view of the political system of the United States in the early 1800s?

6. How strong is Historian A's interpretation?

[Continued on next page.]

[Continued from previous page.]

Historian B

7. What is the main point of Historian B's interpretation?

8. Evaluate the reasoning used in the last sentence of the first paragraph.

9. Evaluate the reasoning used in the third and fourth paragraphs.

10. Evaluate one piece of evidence used to support this interpretation.

11. How strong is Historian B's interpretation?

UNIT 3
Slavery

LESSON 10 Identifying and Evaluating Evidence

Identifying Evidence

Label each item below with the appropriate letter.

S A **source** of information is given.

N **No** source of information is given.

_______1. A review in the *Chicago Herald* said the play *West Side Story* was outstanding.

_______2. The Silver Diner is much better than the Grease Pit Restaurant.

_______3. Hinton Helper wrote in his book, *The Impending Crisis in the South*, that the South should do away with slavery.

_______4. Nat Turner led a slave revolt in 1861 in Virginia. Some 60 whites were killed in the revolt.

_______5. Cotton was the most important crop in the South before the Civil War.

_______6. Slavery hurt the entire country according to an article in the *Atlantic Monthly* in 1857.

_______7. Despite attempts to establish cotton mills, the South remained dominated by agriculture. In 1860 the South produced less than 10 percent of the nation's manufactured goods.

Evaluating Evidence

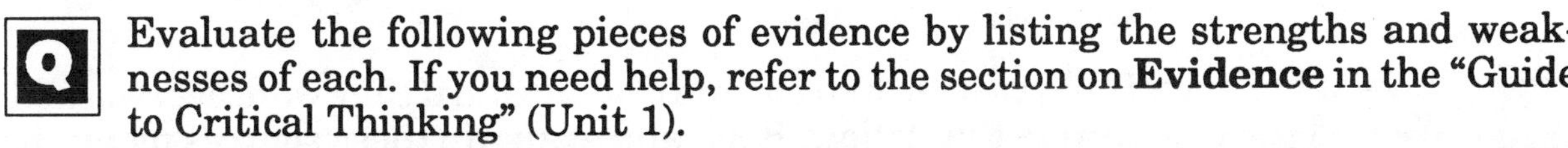

Evaluate the following pieces of evidence by listing the strengths and weaknesses of each. If you need help, refer to the section on **Evidence** in the "Guide to Critical Thinking" (Unit 1).

8. Henry Wilson says in his book, *History of the Rise and Fall of the Slave Power in America* (1875), that slavery reduced men to animals. Wilson was a Radical Republican Senator from Massachusetts. Radical Republicans believed that blacks (now freedmen due to the Thirteenth Amendment, which ended slavery) should be helped by the government, and given equal rights.

   STRENGTHS WEAKNESSES

[Continued on next page.]

[Continued from previous page.]

9. We want to know if slave families were divided by being sold separately to different owners. The slave Maria Perkins wrote a letter in 1852 to her husband, Richard Perkins, telling him that her master sold their son Albert to a slave trader, and soon she might be sold to a different area also.

STRENGTHS WEAKNESSES

10. We want to know if slaves on slave ships tried to commit suicide rather than continue the voyage to become slaves in America. A slave wrote a book, published in 1791, about his life as a slave. In it he says he thought about jumping overboard to drown and that the whites guarded the ship to prevent slaves from jumping over the side.

STRENGTHS WEAKNESSES

Evaluating Sources

We want to know if slaves were well fed and clothed and if they were overworked. We find the two sources that follow. Read and evaluate these sources using the criteria you learned for evaluating sources.

11. Frederick Douglass had been a slave but escaped to freedom and became an abolitionist. In his autobiography he describes his experiences as a slave on a Maryland plantation.

> "...The men and women slaves on Col. Lloyd's farm received their monthly allowance of food, eight pounds of pickled pork, or its equivalent in fish. The pork was often tainted, and the fish were of the poorest quality. With their pork or fish, they had given them one bushel of Indian meal,...of which fifteen percent was more fit for pigs than for men. With this, one pint of salt was

[Continued on next page.]

[Continued from previous page.]

given, and this was the entire monthly allowance of a full-grown slave, working constantly in the open field from morning til night every day except Sunday....The yearly allowance of clothing was not more ample than the supply of food. It consisted of two tow-linen shirts, one pair of trousers of the same course material for summer, and a woolen pair of trousers and a woolen jacket for winter, with one pair of yarn stockings and a pair of shoes...."

STRENGTHS WEAKNESSES

12. Sir Charles Lyell was a well-educated member of an upper-class English family. He travelled to the United States several times in the 1840s and early 1850s. Here he describes slave life on a Georgia plantation.

"...The laborers [slaves] begin work at six o'clock in the morning, have an hour's rest at nine for breakfast, and many have finished their assigned task by two o'clock, all of them by three o'clock. In summer they divide their work differently, going to bed in the middle of the day, then rising to finish their task, and afterward spending a great part of the night in chatting, merry-making, preaching, and psalm-singing....

"...The laborers [slaves] are allowed Indian meal, rice, and milk, and occasionally pork and soup. As their rations are more than they can eat, they either return part of it to the overseer, who makes them an allowance of money for it at the end of the week, or they keep it to feed their fowls, which they usually sell, as well as their eggs, for cash to buy molasses, tobacco, and other luxuries...."

STRENGTHS WEAKNESSES

LESSON 11 Assessing Cause and Effect

Identifying Cause and Effect

Refer to the section on **cause and effect** (pp. 5–6) in the "Guide to Critical Thinking" (Unit 1).

Q Label each item below with the appropriate letter.

C The item involves **cause-and-effect** reasoning.

N The item does **not** involve cause-and-effect reasoning.

_______1. Most people enjoy eating dessert.

_______2. The movie "Terminator 2" was very popular all over the country.

_______3. Sunbathing may get you a tan, but it may also lead to skin cancer.

_______4. Jane, a slave on a Virginia plantation, ran away after her owner whipped her. She couldn't put up with being whipped.

_______5. Many slaves escaped through the underground railroad, an organized set of escape routes in which runaways stayed in people's homes. Once it was set up, more slaves escaped.

_______6. The Liberty Party took votes away from the Whigs in the 1844 election, and thereby helped the Democrat James K. Polk get elected.

_______7. A significant number of abolitionists were young adults from rich New England families.

Evaluating Cause and Effect

The key questions for evaluating cause and effect are

- Is there a good connection between the cause and the effect?
- Are there other possible causes?

[Continued on next page.]

[Continued from previous page.]

Use the key questions to help you evaluate how strong the cause-and-effect reasoning is in the statements below. Explain your reasoning.

8. The famous abolitionist William Lloyd Garrison was very critical of Northerners who were not actively trying to end slavery. As a result of Garrison's criticisms, many Northerners became angry with and hostile to abolitionists, which hurt the abolitionist cause.

9. Nat Turner's Revolt in 1831 sent shock waves of fear throughout the South. After 1831 Southern legislatures passed stricter slave codes that limited the actions of slaves as well as free blacks. The codes also made it more difficult for planters (slave owners) to free their slaves.

LESSON 12 Analyzing Generalizations

Identifying Generalizations

Refer to the section on **generalizations** (pp. 8–11) in the "Guide to Critical Thinking" (Unit 1) for help. Pay special attention to the cue words for identifying generalizations.

Q Label each item below with the appropriate letter.

G The item involves a **generalization**.

N The item does **not** involve a generalization.

_______1. Left-handed people tend to be more creative than right-handed people.

_______2. Most of the players showed up for practice on Tuesday.

_______3. Mexico borders the United States.

_______4. Slaves worked very hard on large plantations.

_______5. Forty-five percent of married slaves who registered in Nelson County, Virginia said they were married less than ten years.

_______6. Nat Turner led a slave rebellion in Virginia in 1831.

_______7. Nat Turner's rebellion caused most Southerners to become more fearful of slaves.

Evaluating Generalizations

The key question for evaluating generalizations is

- How large and representative is the sample?

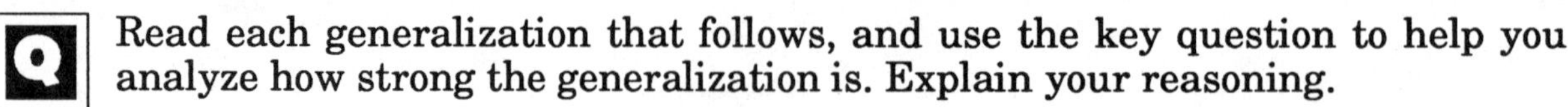

Q Read each generalization that follows, and use the key question to help you analyze how strong the generalization is. Explain your reasoning.

8. Most slaves in the United States worked hard because they had opportunities to

[Continued on next page.]

[Continued from previous page.]

move up to better jobs on the plantations if they did well. This is shown in the records of 33 estates in the South. On these plantations, 7% of the slave men held management positions, 12% were skilled craftsmen, and another 7.4% were in semiskilled jobs or were house servants. Thus, there were real opportunities for hardworking field hands to move to better jobs.

9. After 1831, many Southern states outlawed teaching slaves to read and write.

10. The birth records of a large South Carolina plantation, kept over approximately 100 years, included the names of both mother and father. The records show that on this plantation, most slaves lived in long marriages.

11. Census takers in 1860 were instructed to take down the name, age, sex, occupation, and other information about any slave that had died during the previous year. The census takers in 13 of Mississippi's 60 counties, 59 of Georgia's 132 counties, and 19 of South Carolina's 30 districts faithfully reported all the information on a total of more than 4200 dead slaves of both sexes. These 3 states produced almost half of the cotton crop in 1860, and they contained one-third of the South's slaves. The records show that on cotton plantations, at least, the vast majority of slaves were field hands. Moreover, very few slaves changed position. That is, if you started as a field hand, you would very likely work your whole adult life as a field hand.

LESSON 13 Identifying and Assessing Types of Reasoning

Identify the type of reasoning used in each item below and then evaluate that type of reasoning by asking and answering the appropriate question(s). Each item may contain more than one type of reasoning. Focus your evaluation on the type of reasoning that is most central to the argument. Make diagrams to assist your evaluation when you think they would be helpful.

The types of reasoning and key questions are

Cause-and-effect—Is there a reasonable connection between cause and effect?
—Are there other possible causes for this effect?
Comparison—How are the two cases similar and different?
Generalization—How large and representative is the sample?

1. Willie forgot to wash his new jeans, so he had to wear his old jeans to school on Friday.

   Type of reasoning:

   Evaluation:

2. Southerners opposed internal improvements (such as government roads) because they feared that such federal government projects would provide a precedent for interfering within a state in other ways, too. The federal government might start interfering with slavery.

   Type of reasoning:

   Evaluation:

3. Not all slaves were badly treated, and not all worked hard. Nor did they all work in fields. Some were house servants, while others were skilled artisans—carpenters, metalworkers, and the like. But most slaves were field hands who were forced to work very hard.

   Type of reasoning:

   Evaluation:

[Continued on next page.]

[Continued from previous page.]

4. The South paid a high price for slavery. All craftsmen and farmers received less for their labor because of the competition of slaves. The capital that might have gone into commerce or industry was tied up in slaves. As a result, the South remained an agricultural community dependent on the North for many of its manufactured goods.

   Type of reasoning:

   Evaluation:

5. Everyone in the South was affected by the plantation economy.

   Type of reasoning:

   Evaluation:

6. The tobacco plantations of Kentucky and Missouri were more productive, due to their fertile soil, than the tobacco plantations of Virginia and Maryland.

   Type of reasoning:

   Evaluation:

7. Many slaves became active Christians to make their own world understandable and their own communities a little independent of the white world.

   Type of reasoning:

   Evaluation:

8. White workers in Southern cities and factories did not want to work alongside blacks.

   Type of reasoning:

   Evaluation:

LESSON 14 Was Slavery Good or Bad?

In this lesson you'll read viewpoints written before the Civil War defending and attacking slavery in the South. They have been summarized and edited. Read them and answer the questions.

Viewpoint A

(1) It has been the practice in all countries and in all ages, in some degree, to develop the type of government according to the wants, intelligence, and moral levels of the nations or individuals to be governed. A highly moral and intellectual people, like the free citizens of ancient Athens, are best governed by a democracy. Now, it is clear that Athenian democracy would not suit a Negro nation, nor will the government of mere law suffice for the individual Negro. He is but a grown-up child, and must be governed as a child. The master occupies towards him the place of parent or guardian.

(2) Secondly, the Negro is extravagant; he will not lay up in summer for the wants of winter; he will not accumulate in youth for the needs of old age. He would become an insufferable burden to society. Society has the right to prevent this, and can only do so by subjecting him to domestic slavery.

(3) In the last place, the Negro race is inferior to the white race, and living in their midst, they would be far outstripped or outwitted in the chase of free competition. Gradual but certain extermination would be their fate.

(4) Those who criticize Negro slavery should remember that slavery here relieves the Negro from a far more cruel slavery in Africa, or from idolatry (false religions) and cannibalism, and every brutal vice and crime that can disgrace humanity; and that it Christianizes, protects, supports and civilizes him; that it governs him far better than free laborers in the North are governed. There, wife-murder has become a mere holiday pastime; and where so many wives are murdered, almost all must be brutally treated. Nay more: men who kill their wives or treat them brutally, must be ready for all kinds of crimes, and the calendar of crime in the North proves the inference to be correct. Negroes never kill their wives. If it be objected that legally they have no wives, then we reply, that in an experience of more than forty years, we never yet heard of a Negro man killing a Negro woman. Our Negroes are not only better off as to physical comforts than free laborers, but their moral condition is better.

[Continued on next page.]

[Continued from previous page.]

Viewpoint A

1. What is the main point of Viewpoint A?

2. Review the explanation of fallacies (errors in reasoning) on pages 6, 10–12, and 14. Then from the list of fallacies below, choose at least 3 fallacies committed in Viewpoint A. Write the fallacy, and explain the part of the argument (paragraph and phrase) where the fallacy occurs, and how the author committed that fallacy.

Single cause (p. 6)
Preceding event as cause (p. 6)
Correlation as cause (p. 6)
False Scenario (p. 6)
Hasty generalization (p. 10)
Composition/stereotyping (p. 10)
Prevalent proof (p. 12)
Negative proof (p. 12)
Special pleading (p. 11)
Golden mean (p. 13)
Either-or (p. 14)

	Location (Paragraph/phrase)	Fallacy	Explanation
a.			
b.			
c.			

[Continued from previous page.]

3. Evaluate the evidence this author presents.

4. Do you think George Fitzhugh, the author of Viewpoint A, believed what he wrote in this argument?

5. In another writing, George Fitzhugh wrote that human bonds are closer in family ties. People act out of trust, generosity, and love. On the other hand, capitalism, such as in factories, is impersonal and based on greed. Slavery is a closer approximation to family than to capitalism, so it is a superior system for organizing society. Government should be based on the social ties emphasized in slavery. Evaluate this argument.

Viewpoint B

(1) Several million persons in the Southern States are held as slaves by force and fear, and for no crime! Reader, what do you think of such treatment? Suppose I should kidnap you, take your liberty away, and make you work in my fields without pay for as long as you live? Everybody knows that slaveholders do these very things to the slaves all the time. Yet some people say that the slaveholders treat the slaves kindly, that they love their slaves and never are cruel to them.

(2) We will prove by a thousand witnesses that the slaves are whipped with such inhuman severity, as to lacerate and mangle their flesh in the most shocking manner, leaving permanent scars; after establishing this, we will present a mass of testimony, concerning a great variety of other tortures. The testimony, for the most part, will be that of the slaveholders themselves, and in their own chosen words. A large portion of it will be taken from the advertisements, which they have published in their own newspapers, describing, by the scars on their bodies made by the whip, their own runaway slaves. In the column under the word *witnesses*, will be found the name of the individual, who signs the advertisement, or for

[Continued on next page.]

Viewpoint B

[Continued from previous page.]

whom it is signed, with his or her place of residence, and the name and date of the paper in which it appeared, and generally the name of the place where it is published. Opposite the name of each witness will be an extract, from the advertisement, containing his or her testimony.

Witnesses	Testimony
Mr. D. Judd, jailor, Davidson Co., Tennessee, in the *Nashville Banner* , Dec. 10, 1838	"Committed to jail as a runaway, a negro woman named Martha, 17 or 18 years of age, has *numerous scars of the whip* on her back."
Mr. Robert Nicoll, Dauphin St. between Emmanuel and Conception St.s, Mobile, Alabama, in the *Mobile Commercial Advertiser*	"Ten dollars reward for my woman Siby, *very much scarred about the neck and ears by whipping* ."
Mr. Bryant Johnson, Fort Valley, Houston Co., Georgia, in the *Standard of Union*, Milledgeville, Ga., Oct. 2, 1838	"Ranaway, a negro woman, named Maria, *some scars on her back occasioned by the whip* ."
Mr. James T. De Jarnett, Vernon, Autauga Co., Alabama, in the *Pensacola Gazette*, July 14, 1838	"Stolen a negro woman, named Celia. On examining her back you will find *marks caused by the whip* ."
Maurice Y. Garcia, Sheriff of the County of Jefferson, La., in the *New Orleans Bee*, August 14, 1838	"Lodged in jail, a mulatto boy, *having large marks of the whip*, on his shoulders and other parts of his body."
Mr. Asa B. Metcalf, Kingston, Adams Co., Mi. in the *Natchez Courier*, June 15, 1832	"Ranaway Mary, a black woman, has a *scar* on her back and right arm near the shoulder, *caused by a rifle ball* ."
Mr. William Overstreet, Benton, Yazoo Co., Mi., in the *Lexington (Kentucky) Observer*, July 22, 1838	"Ranaway a negro man named Henry, *his left eye out,* some scars from a *dirk* on and under his left arm, and *much scarred with the whip* ."
Mr. R.P. Carney, Clark Co., Ala., in the *Mobile Register*, Dec. 22, 1832	"One hundred dollars reward for a negro fellow Pompey, 40 years old, he is *branded on the left jaw* .

[Continued on next page.]

[Continued from previous page.]

Viewpoint B

6. What is the main point of Viewpoint B?

7. Evaluate the reasoning used in the following:
   a. Last sentence of first paragraph

   b. First sentence of second paragraph

8. What is the possible fallacy in the fourth sentence of the first paragraph? ("Everybody knows...") Hint: It is one of those listed on pages 12 and 13.

9. Evaluate one of the sources presented to support Viewpoint B. Use at least four criteria for evaluating sources.

10. Assume that all these pieces of evidence are reliable. How convincing is it that cruelty to slaves was widespread?

LESSON 15 How Did Slavery Affect Slaves?

Background Information

Slavery in the United States existed for almost two hundred years from about 1670 to 1865.

Slavery does not mean quite the same thing at different times in history or in different places. In the United States, a slave was different from a servant in two important ways: (1) slaves were slaves for life, unless their owners emancipated them, and (2) the children of slaves were also slaves.

Not all historians agree with this characterization of slavery; nevertheless, it gives you a general idea of what you are studying.

Historians have studied many different issues about slavery, often resulting in lengthy scholarly debates. For example, historians have argued about whether slavery was still profitable by 1860.

You will read two interpretations about the conditions of slavery and how those conditions affected slaves. Read the interpretations, and carefully consider the relevant information, then answer the questions that follow.

Historian A (1959)

(1) What were the effects of slavery on slaves? Recent work in social psychology provides insights to this question. An examination of slavery in the United States in relation to Nazi concentration camps also provides greater understanding of the psychological effects of bondage on slaves.

(2) Slave plantations in the United States were like concentration camps in Nazi Germany in many ways. Slave owners, like the guards in concentration camps, had almost complete control over their slaves. Owners could beat their slaves with little worry of punishment by the government. Slaves in the United States had no civil rights, right to marry, right to own property, or any other rights.[1] Slaves could not leave the plantations without the permission of their owners or overseers, so they were under the absolute control of their overseers.[2]

(3) The result of this total dependence of slaves on their owners was the passive personality so commonly observed among slaves.[3] Slaves passively did whatever they were told. They didn't work hard; they just shuffled around and didn't cause any trouble.

(4) This passive slave personality is the same behavior observed in concentration camp prisoners.[4] The prisoners passively took the cruelties and tortures without resistance. There were few revolts, even when the prisoners were herded into gas chambers.[5]

(5) In summary, slaves in the United States, unlike slaves elsewhere, were under the complete control of their owners. As a result, American slaves became passive and childlike, their personalities crushed under slavery. Domination by slave owners is a key to understanding how bad slavery in the United States really was.

[Continued on next page.]

[Continued from previous page.]

Endnotes for Historian A (Quotation marks indicate direct quote from the source.)

1. William Goodell, *The American Slave Code in Theory and Practice*. (New York: American and Foreign Anti-Slavery Society, 1853), p. 92.

   "A slave is in absolute bondage [in the United States]; he has no civil rights, and can hold no property, except at the will and pleasure of his master."

2. John Codman Hurd, *The Law of Freedom and Bondage in The United States*. (Boston: Little, Brown, 1958), Vol. I, p. 232.

   "Should a white man be attacked by a slave and be injured or maimed, the punishment was automatically death. A 1669 Virginia law declared it not a serious crime if a master or overseer killed a slave who resisted punishment."

3. Samuel Eliot Morison and Henry Steele Commager, *The Growth of the American Republic*. (New York: Oxford University Press, 1950), Vol. I, p. 537.

   "[The average slave was] childlike, improvident, humorous, prevaricating, and superstitious...."

   "The 'Sambo' [passive, childlike] stereotype appears in far too many different pieces of literature and in much too detailed a form for it to be made up. There must have been Sambo slaves."

4. Bruno Bettleheim, "Individual and Mass Behavior in Extreme Situations," *Journal of Abnormal Psychology*, XXXVIII (October, 1943), p. 141.

   "The prisoners developed types of behavior which are characteristic of infancy or early youth."

5. Eugene Kogon, *The Theory and Practice of Hell*. (New York: Farrar, Straus, 1946), p. 284.

   "With a few altogether insignificant exceptions, the prisoners, no matter in what form they were led to execution, whether singly, in groups, or in masses, never fought back!"

Historian B (1974)

(1) Slavery in the United States has been subjected to close study by historians. The accepted view is that slavery was extremely bad. Supporters of this position argue that in addition to depriving slaves of their freedom, slave owners treated slaves brutally, dominated them into passive personalities, and prevented them from getting the basic necessities of life—food, clothing, and shelter. The accepted view exaggerates the bad aspects of slavery, however. Slavery did, of course, deprive millions of humans of freedom. But generally, slaves were treated well by their masters.

(2) Previous historians have been incorrect in their view of slavery because they haven't examined enough information. My viewpoint is more accurate because I have used computers to analyze mountains of statistical information about slavery in the South. The use of computers in this way marks the beginning of a scientifically objective view of slavery.

(3) The belief by some historians that slaves did not get the basic necessities of food, clothing, and shelter is mistaken. Slaves ate a diet which gave them 100% of the Recommended Daily Allowance (RDA) for all nutrients.[1] Their clothing was as good as freemen's clothing of the same time period. And slave housing was also as good as, or better than, housing for free people. The typical slave house was 18 by 20 feet, which provided more sleeping space than New York City workers had in 1893.[2]

[Continued on next page.]

Historian B

[Continued from previous page.]

(4) Slaves were sometimes whipped, but in general, they were not physically punished. The idea that slave owners relied on the whip alone to get slaves to work hard is a highly misleading myth. The records of Louisiana plantation owner Bennet Barrow show that there were only 0.7 whippings per slave per year. (That is, for every ten slaves on the plantation, there were 7 whippings per year.)[3] Actually, slave owners more often used positive incentives, such as prizes, year-end bonuses, or grants of land to get slaves to work hard.

(5) As a result of the incentives, slaves identified with their masters and worked very hard. Slaves were more efficient than free white farm workers in the North at that time. Plantations had greater output per worker per year than Northern farms.[4] (That is, a slave might be responsible for the production of 1,000 bushels of a crop per year, while a Northern white farm worker might have an output of 900 bushels per year.)

(6) Overall, although slavery deprived slaves of freedom, it also provided adequate food, clothing, and shelter. Slave owners did not often beat their slaves. Rather, slaves cooperated with their owners in a highly efficient system to produce a large volume of crops. The effects of freeing slaves after the Civil War shows that slavery had not been that bad. It was quickly apparent that blacks were physically worse off as freedmen than they had been as slaves.

Endnotes for Historian B

1. The nutritional value of the slave diet: average daily slave consumption of various nutrients in 1860 as a percentage of modern recommended daily allowances—calculation done by Historian B. (Note: 100% would be all a person would need of the nutrient for a day.)

Nutrient	Percent	Nutrient	Percent
Protein	212%	Thiamine	475%
Calcium	120%	Riboflavin	151%
Iron	338%	Niacin	173%
Vitamin A	1270%	Vitamin C	252%

2. US Bureau of Labor Special Report, *The Slums of Baltimore, Chicago, New York, and Philadelphia*, 1894, pp. 12, 23–24.
3. From the diary of Bennet H. Barrow, 1840–1842. His plantation numbered about 200 slaves, of whom about 120 were in the labor force. The record shows that over the course of two years a total of 160 whippings were administered, or 80 each year. About half the workers were not whipped at all during the two-year period.
4. Southern agriculture as a whole was about 35% more efficient than Northern agriculture in 1860. Southern slave farms were 28% more efficient than Southern free farms.

[Continued on next page.]

[Continued from previous page.]

Relevant Information

1. The slave population in the United States increased by reproduction. That is, on average more slaves were born than died each year. In other slave societies in the New World (for example, in Cuba, Haiti, and Jamaica) slaves did not live long enough to replace themselves. Slaves had to be replaced by the slave trade from Africa.
2. Concentration camps were set up by the German Nazi Party under Adolf Hitler. The main purpose of concentration camps was to kill people. Eventually concentration camps were used to accomplish Hitler's "final solution," the extermination (killing) of all Jews in Europe.
3. In concentration camps people were herded into large barracks with very unsanitary conditions. The guards were not concerned if people died of diseases (as long as the guards didn't get the diseases).
4. Torture and brutality were a regular feature of concentration camps. Often it was arbitrary—people were picked at random to be tortured.
5. Millions of people died in concentration camps.
6. Whether or not slave marriages were regarded as legal, slaves lived in family units. That is, a husband, wife, and children lived together.
7. Many slaves were house servants, nannies, or skilled workers (e.g., carpenters, coopers, blacksmiths), although most slaves were field hands, picking cotton or other plantation crops.
8. Most slaves lived on farms and plantations of less than 20 slaves. On these farms, slaves worked with and knew their owners well.
9. The efficiency of workers is measured in terms of productivity, which is calculated as output per worker per hour.
10. The South has a longer growing season than the North.
11. A whipping could be a brutal beating, although owners were cautious not to go too far for fear of killing or maiming their slaves, thus ruining their investment.

Historian A

1. What is the main point of Historian A?

[Continued on next page.]

[Continued from previous page.]

2. Evaluate these two pieces of evidence. (Remember to make an overall judgment of each.)

   a. Endnote 1—

   b. Endnote 3—

3. Identify the reasoning (cause and effect, comparison, or generalization) in the first sentence of the second paragraph, and then evaluate it. (The questions for evaluating each type of reasoning are listed at the bottom of page 18.)

4. Evaluate the cause-and-effect reasoning in the second and third paragraphs.

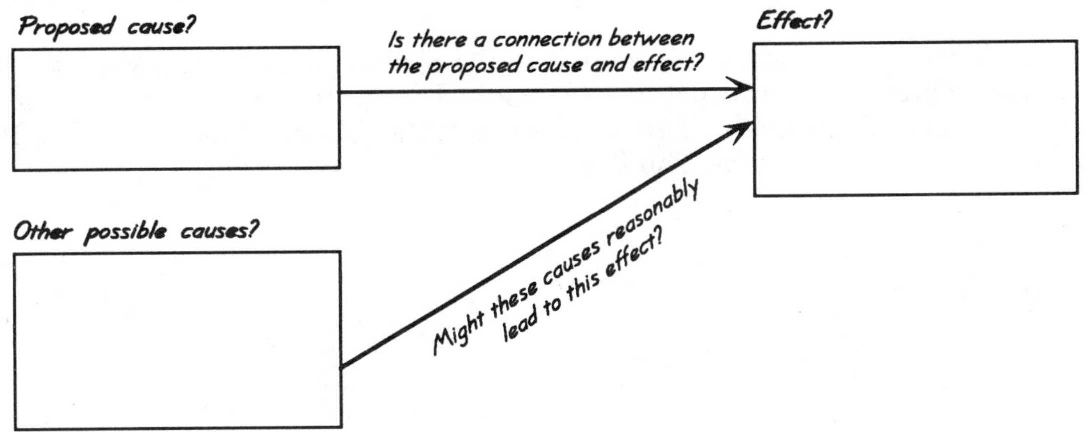

5. Overall, how strong is Historian A's interpretation?

[Continued on next page.]

[Continued from previous page.]

Historian B

6. What is the main point of Historian B?

7. What is missing from Endnote 1 that would help us to better evaluate it?

8. What fallacy does Historian B commit in the second paragraph in saying, "My viewpoint is more accurate because I have used computers to analyze mountains of statistical information..."? Hint: It is one of the fallacies found on pages 10–12 of the "Guide to Critical Thinking" (Unit 1).

9. In the last two sentences in paragraph 3, Historian B compares slave housing to free housing. Evaluate that comparison. Take special note of Endnote 2.

[Continued on next page.]

[Continued from previous page.]

10. Identify and evaluate the reasoning used in the third sentence of paragraph 4.

11. Identify and evaluate the reasoning used in the fifth paragraph, after the first sentence.

12. Identify and evaluate the reasoning used in the last two sentences in paragraph 6.

13. Overall, how strong is Historian B's interpretation?

[Continued on next page.]

[Continued from previous page.]

Excerpt from *Uncle Tom's Cabin*

by Harriet Beecher Stowe, pp. 353, 364–66

(Uncle Tom and some other slaves are riding with their new owner, Simon Legree, to his plantation.)

"Ye see what ye'd get!" said (Simon) Legree, caressing the dogs with grim satisfaction, and turning to Tom and his companions. "Ye see what ye'd get, if ye try to run off. These yer dogs has been raised to track niggers; and they'd jest as soon chaw one of ye up as eat their supper. So mind yerself!"...

These two colored men (Sambo and Quimbo) were the two principal hands on the plantation. Legree had trained them in savageness and brutality as systematically as he had his bulldogs; and by long practice in hardness and cruelty, brought their whole nature to about the same range of capacities....

(At the end of the day the slaves are bringing in the cotton they picked to be weighed.)

Slowly the weary, dispirited creatures wound their way into the room, and, with crouching reluctance, presented their baskets to be weighed.

Legree noted on a slate, on the side of which was pasted a list of names, the amount.

Tom's basket was weighed and approved; and he looked with anxious glance, for the success of the woman he had befriended.

Tottering with weakness, she came forward, and delivered her basket. It was full weight, as Legree well perceived; but, affecting anger, he said, "What, you lazy beast! Short again! Stand aside, you'll catch it, pretty soon!"

The woman gave a groan of utter despair, and sat on a board....

"And now," said Legree, "come here, you Tom. You see, I telled ye I didn't buy ye jest for the common work; I mean to promote ye, and make a driver of ye; and to-night ye may jest as well begin to get yer hand in. Now, ye jest take this yer gal and flog her; ye've seen enough on't to know how."

"I beg Mas'rs pardon," said Tom, "hopes Mas'r won't set me at that. It's what I an't used to—never did—and can't do, no way possible....I'm willin' to work night and day, and work while there's life and breath in me; but this yer thing I can't feel it right to do;—and Mas'r, I <u>never</u> shall do it—<u>never</u>!"

Legree looked stupefied and confounded; but at last burst forth,—

"What! ye blasted black beast! Tell <u>me</u> ye don't think it <u>right</u> to do what I tell ye! What have any of you cussed cattle to do with thinking what's right!...Here you rascal, you make believe to be so pious—didn't you never hear, out of yer Bible, 'servants, obey your masters?' An't I yer master? Didn't I pay down twelve hundred dollars, cash, for all there is inside yer old cussed black shell? An't yer

[Continued on next page.]

Uncle Tom's Cabin

[Continued from previous page.]

mine, now, body and soul?" he said, giving Tom a violent kick with his heavy boot; "tell me!"

"No! No! No! my soul an't yours, Mas'r! You haven't bought it,—ye can't buy it! It's been bought and paid for, by one that is able to keep it; no matter, no matter, you can't harm me."

"I can't!" said Legree, with a sneer; "we'll see—we'll see! Here, Sambo, Quimbo, give this dog such a breakin' in as he won't get over, this month!"

The two gigantic Negroes that now laid hold of Tom, with fiendish exultation in their faces, might have formed no unapt personification of powers of darkness. The poor woman screamed with apprehension, and all rose, as by a general impulse, while they dragged him unresisting from the place.

Excerpt from *Gone with the Wind*

by Margaret Mitchell, pp. 22–23

(This excerpt describes Mammy, a slave of the O'Hara family.)

Scarlet heard Mammy's lumbering tread shaking the floor....It would never do for Mammy to suspect that anything was wrong. Mammy felt that she owned the O'Haras, body and soul, that their secrets were her secrets; and even a hint of a mystery was enough to set her upon the trail as relentlessly as a bloodhound....

Mammy emerged from the hall, a huge woman with the small shrewd eyes of an elephant. She was shining black, pure African, devoted to her last drop of blood to the O'Haras....Mammy was black, but her code of conduct and her sense of pride were as high as or higher than that of her owners....Whom Mammy loved, she chastened. And, as her love for Scarlet and her pride in her were enormous, the chastening process was practically continuous.

LESSON 16 What Was It Like to Be a Slave?

Background Information

Slaves in the United States, unlike indentured servants, were slaves for life (unless emancipated by their owners), and their children were also slaves. Slavery lasted for almost 200 years in the United States, from about 1670 to 1865.

Three interpretations of slavery are presented in this lesson. Read them, along with the endnotes and relevant information, and then answer the questions that follow.

Historian A (1959)

(1) Historians have debated the evils of slavery for generations. James Ford Rhodes (1893) described it as a curse to both master and slave. Ulrich B. Phillips (1918) countered that the evils of slavery were wildly exaggerated. He emphasized the humane friendship between kind-hearted master and contented, faithful, and childlike slaves. Kenneth Stampp (1956) reasserted the traditional view, showing the harshness and cruelty of the system. My interpretation makes a fresh examination of slavery through the lens of social psychology to provide a new perspective to the old debate on the evils of slavery, and it provides insights into the behavior of slaves and masters.

(2) Basically, slavery in the United States was much worse than slavery in other countries and had a much more severe effect on the slaves. American slavery was comparable in many ways to a concentration camp. It took away personal initiative from slaves and destroyed their personalities.

(3) Unlike slavery elsewhere, slavery in the United States had no institutions, such as the church or government, to either oppose the slave owners, or to control slavery for the benefit of the slaves.[1] Slave owners had complete dominance over their slaves. In contrast to relatively "open" systems of slavery in other countries, slavery in the United States was a "closed" system. This contrast can be illustrated by comparing the slave systems in Latin America and the United States.

(4) In Latin America slavery was a relatively "open" system. Slaves there had certain rights and some possibilities to develop themselves personally.[2] The Catholic Church and the mercantile governments of the European Powers ruling the Latin American countries intervened frequently in the slave system.[3] The slave owner had to be conscious of the clergy and government officials in his dealings with his slaves. As a result, the harshness of slavery was softened considerably.

(5) Slaves in Latin America were not automatically slaves forever; they could purchase their own freedom.[4] Slaves were thought to have immortal souls and, as such, were to be

[Continued on next page.]

Historian A

[Continued from pervious page.]

legally married and receive the sacraments.[5] Masters' disciplinary power over slaves was limited by the laws of the government. Masters were liable for the murder of their slaves.[6] Although the law was violated, and owners were sometimes cruel to their slaves, the laws were not as widely violated as they were under the English or in the United States.[7] Government officials and priests regularly checked to see if slaves had been mistreated. Slaves could also own property. Lastly, slaves in Latin America regularly had contacts with the rest of society.[8] One of the results of this was a much higher rate of intermarriage than in the United States.

(6) By contrast, slavery in the United States was a "closed" system. Slaves had almost no rights and were totally dependent upon their master for nearly everything.[9] The term of servitude in the United States was for life; slaves couldn't buy their freedom.[10] There was no recognition of marriage or the family. Slaves were to be sold to the highest bidder even if it meant breaking up the family.[11] Conversion to Christianity meant no difference in status or treatment as slaves.[12] Slaves as property took precedence over slaves as human beings.[13] They had no civil rights, right to own property, or any other rights.[14] Slaves were limited to the plantation—they had little contact with the rest of society. They were isolated on the plantation under the absolute control of their owners, to whom they were to give complete obedience.[15] The masters exercised such extensive power because there were no governmental restrictions on them.[16]

(7) The result of the closed system of slavery in the United States was to destroy the personality of the slave; that is, to reduce his behavior to that of a child. Historians have long noticed the passive personality among slaves.[17] Many slaves were docile, irresponsible people, perpetual children incapable of mature behavior. Slaves passively did whatever they were told. They had no initiative, and offered no resistance to slavery. Some people have contended that this is just another white stereotype of blacks, yet abundant evidence proves that the passive personality type did exist in the United States.

(8) Since there is no evidence of the passive personality in slavery in Latin America, one is left with the conclusion that the passive personality must be the result of the authoritarian nature of American slavery. The absolute power of the slave owners over their slaves, but not necessarily the cruelty of the masters, was enough to produce passive slaves.

(9) Many of the blacks brought from Africa to the United States as slaves had been warriors or had held high positions in their advanced civilizations.[18] They were transformed into passive people as a result of their enslavement. There was the shock of being caught and enslaved, and the several-week march to the coast. The next shock was their sale to the Europeans. They were put into pens and branded. Blacks rejected as slaves were left to starve.[19] The cruelest step was the middle passage on slave ships across the Atlantic Ocean. Slaves were packed in and chained down in the

[Continued on next page.]

Historian A

[Continued from previous page.]

hold of the ships for two months, where they remained amidst their own vomit and excrement.[20] If they survived this ordeal they were introduced to severe masters and conditions in the West Indies. Then they were transported and sold to owners in the United States. By this time two-thirds of the slaves had died.[21]

(10) After all these shocks to their personalities, slaves could not be expected to exhibit aggressive behavior. They had to look for new cues for the type of behavior expected of them in America. Since the master had complete control and authority, the only person the slave could look to was the master. The master became like a father. The result was the childlike personality dependent upon the master.

(11) With this dependent personality of slaves in the United States, there was little chance for organized revolt against the slave owners. Whereas there were many slave revolts in Latin America, some of them amounting to full-scale wars, there were very few in the United States. Moreover, the few revolts in the United States were led by non-slaves.[22] This phenomenon supports the view that slaves in Latin America retained much of their personalities, including their will to resist.

(12) The striking aspect of slavery in the United States, and especially the passive personality, is its similarity to personality changes in concentration camps under Hitler's Germany. Like the slave owners, the guards (called SS) had absolute power over the inmates. Even though they were brutal, the SS became father figures to the prisoners, since they were the only figures of authority. Inmates accepted the values of the SS, and most inmates did not hate the SS when they were released—they showed no emotion.[23]

(13) Brutalities were so great in concentration camps that inmates soon felt that the brutalities were not happening to them. They testified years later that they had felt separate from their bodies. The tortures were happening to their bodies, but not to them. It was like watching someone else being tortured. The unreal self became the real self.[24] There were few cases of resistance to the guards or revolts in concentration camps, even when they were being herded into gas chambers! There were few cases of suicide—the inmates had completely passive personalities.[25]

(14) It is obvious that there are striking parallels between personality traits exhibited in concentration camps and in slavery in the United States. The effects of slavery in the United States on blacks were profound. Their personalities were destroyed, and, as such, their ability to form meaningful relationships and families was destroyed. Since these awful consequences did not exist in slavery elsewhere, the conclusion is inescapable that it was the unchecked and complete power of the slave owners, the closed nature of the system in the United States, which led to the childlike, passive personality.

[Continued on next page.]

[Continued from previous page.]

Endnotes For Historian A

Quotation marks indicate a direct quote from the source. Other entries are a summary of the source.

1. Richard Hildreth, *The History of the United States of America* (New York: Harper), 1858, Vol. VI, p. 597.
2. Sir Harry Johnston, *The Negro in the New World* (London: Methuen, 1910), p. 89.

   "Slavery under the flag of Portugal [in Brazil] or of Spain was not a condition without hope, a life in hell, as it was for the most part in the British West Indies and, above all, Dutch Guiana and the Southern United States."
3. Fernando Ortiz, *Los Negros Esckavis* (Havana: Revista bimestra Cuban, 1916) pp. 334–35.

   In Spain and Spanish colonies there was a body of law governing slavery, while in the English colonies (including the United States) there was no pre-existing law. "Perhaps it is due to this circumstance that the slave legislation of the English colonies (including the United States) was more severe than the Spanish, and that the master's power to which the slave was subjected in the former was more absolute and uncontrollable."
4. William Law Mathieson, *British Slavery and Its Abolition* (London: Longmans, Green, 1926), pp. 37–38.

   "In the Cuban market, freedom was the only commodity which could be bought untaxed; every negro against whom no one had proved a claim of servitude was deemed free."
5. Johnston, p. 43

   "According to the first item of the Spanish code, 'Everyone who has slaves is obliged to instruct them in the principles of the Roman Catholic religion and in the necessary truths in order that the slaves may be baptized within the [first] year of their residence in the Spanish dominions.'"
6. Johnston, pp. 45–46
7. Carl Berns Wadstrom, *An Essay on Colonization…* (London: Darton and Harvey, 1794), p. 151.

   "The Spaniards, Portuguese and Danes are undoubtedly the best masters of slaves." The English and Dutch were, in his opinion, the worst.
8. *Life in Brazil, or the Land of the Cocoa and the Palm* (New York: Harper, 1856), p. 267.

   Thomas Ewbank (an English traveler in Brazil) wrote in the 1850s: "I have passed black ladies in silks and jewelry with male slaves in livery behind them…several with white husbands. The first doctor of the city is a colored man; so is the President of the Province."
9. J. B. D. DeBow, *Industrial Resources* (1852–53), Vol. II, p. 249.

   "On our estates [plantations in the United States] we dispense with the whole machinery of public police and public courts of justice. Thus we try, decide and execute sentences in thousands of cases, which in other countries would go into courts."
10. John Codman Hurd, *The Law of Freedom and Bondage in the United States* (Boston: Little and Brown, 1958), Vol. I, p. 303.

    Slaves in the United States had become "chattels personal." That is, they were totally controlled by their owners.
11. Helen T. Catterall, *Judicial Cases Concerning American Slavery and the Negro* (Washington: Carnegie Institution, 1926), Vol. II, p. 221.

    "…with slaves it [marriage] may be dissolved at the pleasure of either party, or by the sale of one or both, depending on the caprice or necessity of the owners."
12. William Hand Browne (ed.), *Archives of Maryland* (Baltimore, 1844), Vol. II, p. 272.

    Maryland law of 1671 stated that any Christianized slave shall remain a slave.
13. Hurd, Vol. I, p. 42–43.

    "In slavery [in the United States], strictly so called, the supreme power of the state, in ignoring the

[Continued on next page.]

Endnotes for Historian A

[Continued from previous page.]

personality of the slave, ignores his capacity for moral action, and commits the control of his conduct as a moral agent, to the master."

14. William Goodell, *The American Slave Code in Theory and Practice* (New York: American and Foreign Anti-Slavery Society, 1853), p. 92.

    "A slave is in absolute bondage [in the United States]; he has no civil right, and can hold no property, except at the will and pleasure of his master."

15. Hurd, Vol. I, p. 232.

    Should a white man be attacked by a slave and be injured or maimed, the punishment was automatically death. A 1669 Virginia law declared it not a felony (that is, not a serious crime) if a master or overseer killed a slave who resisted punishment.

16. Hurd, Vol. I, pp. 42–43. See the quote in endnote 13.
17. Samuel Eliot Morison and Henry Steel Commager, *The Growth of the American Republic* (New York: Oxford University Press, 1950), Vol. I, p. 537.

    "[The average slave was] childlike, improvident, humorous, prevaricating, and superstitious...."

18. E. F. Ward, *A History of the Gold Coast* (London: George Allen and Unwin, 1948), pp. 107–19. See also C. K. Meek, *Law and Authority in a Nigerian Tribe: A Study in Indirect Rule* (London: Oxford University Press, 1937), pp. 88–164, 206–51.
19. Foxwell Buxton, *Letters on the Slave Trade to the Lord Viscount Melbourne* (London, 1838), pp. 34–38, 41–44.
20. *An Abstract of the Evidence Delivered Before a Select Committee of the House of Commons in the Years 1790 and 1791; on the Part of the Petitioners for the Abolition of the Slave Trade* (London, 1791).
21. Frank Tannenbaum, *Slave and Citizen* (New York: Knopf, 1947), p. 28.
22. Herbert Aptheker, *American Negro Slave Revolts* (New York: Columbia University, 1943), passim.
23. Bruno Bettleheim, "Individual and Mass Behavior in Extreme Situations," *Journal of Abnormal Psychology*, XXXVIII (October, 1943), p. 141.

    "The prisoners developed types of behavior which are characteristic of infancy or early youth."

    Elie Cohen, *Human Behavior in the Concentration Camp* (New York: Norton, 1953), pp. 176–77.

    "Only very few of the prisoners escaped a more or less intensive identification with the S.S. [the guards]. For all of us the S.S. was a father image...."

24. Olga Lengyel, *Five Chimneys: The Story of Auschwitz* (Chicago, 1947), p. 20.

    "I arrived at that state of numbness where I was no longer sensitive to either club or whip. I lived through the rest of that scene as a spectator."

25. Eugene Kogon, *The Theory and Practice of Hell* (New York: Farrar, Straus, 1946), p. 284.

    "With a few altogether insignificant exceptions, the prisoners, no matter what form they were led to execution, whether singly, in groups, or in masses, never fought back!"

Historian B (1972)

(1) Slavery in the Southern United States has been the subject of a great deal of study and debate. Historians have been confronted with some important questions. How bad was slavery in the South? What effect did slavery have on the slave personally and on slaves as families?

(2) Of course, slavery in the South was terrible since it denied freedom to slaves. Nevertheless, there were aspects of it which were not so bad. Slavery in the United States did not crush the personalities or the fami-

[Continued on next page.]

Historian B

[Continued from previous page.]

lies of the slave. Slaves had many ways of resisting total physical and psychological domination, and they were able to maintain their own community.

(3) Other historians have gone wrong in their views of slavery because they did not look at enough evidence by the slaves themselves. Instead, historians have looked more at the views of plantation owners. My interpretation is based primarily on the testimony of slaves and, therefore, views slavery more correctly—through the eyes of those it affected most. While slave narratives must be used with caution, they are important to a more balanced study of the institution of slavery.

(4) The evil involved in slavery is apparent from even a cursory examination. In the voyage to America 16 percent of the slaves died.[1] Suicides and mutinies occurred on voyages, and suicides were not uncommon in America.[2] Enslavement and importation to America destroyed many of the cultural forms and customs of the slaves' advanced societies in Africa.[3] In the United States slaves worked very long hours against their wills, and some masters irrationally flogged (whipped) their slaves.[4]

(5) Not all aspects of slavery were completely bad, however, slaves were allowed to retain their own culture. Many old African customs survived slavery and blended with white American culture, such as music, dance, folk tales, words and idioms, spiritual ideas, voodoo, drums, and funeral rites.[5] The shocks of enslavement and the middle passage (voyage to America) have been exaggerated since most slaves were born in the United States, not imported. Despite some brutalities, most slaves were not tortured or beaten excessively.[6]

(6) Since slaves had their own unique forms of recreation, songs, tales, and religion, they had a significant personal life outside of slavery. These ways promoted group solidarity and prevented total dependence on the master. Slaves engaged in recreation since slave quarters were usually free of white control. Sunday was almost always a day of rest, there were periodic festivals, and slaves could move around at night since night patrols by whites were ineffective.[7] Slave songs expressed their lives (love, work, floggings), made fun of their masters, made folk heroes of rebellious slaves, and provided entertainment.[8] Tales were used to entertain people and to teach children how to survive in slavery. They showed the weaker characters (slaves) outwitting the stronger characters (masters), as in "Brer Rabbit," and often made fools of whites.[9] Masters attempted to control slave religion by stressing, for example, "obey your masters," but when slaves were unsupervised they had their own beliefs. Their God was a personal God of freedom and comfort.[10]

(7) Since slaves in the South could escape total psychological domination, they did not become passive personalities as happened in concentration camps. Blacks captured in Africa were not docile, even with the shock of enslavement.[11] The group solidarity exhibited in America through recreation, songs and other activities, is not seen in concentration camps where each individual was almost totally

[Continued on next page.]

Historian B

[Continued from previous page.]

isolated. Group support helped prevent degeneration into infantile personalities.

(8) That slaves took the initiative to frequently run away shows their will to resist and their lack of infantile, passive personalities. Slaves ran away despite overwhelming odds against them—freedom was the slave's greatest yearning.[12] Some runaways banded together in maroon communities and conducted guerrilla wars against whites. Some of these runaways made alliances with the Seminole Indians.[13] While it is true that there were fewer slave revolts in the United States than in Latin America, this was not due to more passive slaves in America. Rather it was due to high slave-to-white ratios in Latin America (7 to 1 in British West Indies, 11 to 1 in Haiti) and to a shortage of troops there. These factors gave slave revolts a higher probability for success in Latin America.[14]

(9) Actually, there were three stereotyped characters, not just Sambo, in Southern literature on slaves. The most common was Sambo, the faithful, loyal, humorous, dishonest, and docile slave.[15] There were two others, however—Jack and Nat. Jack worked faithfully but only as long as he was not pushed beyond a certain point. He worked only so hard. Nat was a revengeful, bloodthirsty rebel. He defied all the rules of the plantation and was a chronic runaway.[16]

(10) The Sambo stereotype does not accurately describe most slaves. It is a typical unflattering view of the lowest caste in many slave societies throughout history, even in Brazil.[17] It tells us more about the white owners than the slaves. Many whites believed blacks were inferior since it helped relieve them of the burden of thinking of blacks as men. In reality, however, whites did not treat slaves as Samboes. Why did they have such great fear of rebellion if slaves were passive?[18] Constant surveillance was necessary to control slaves. If all slaves were Samboes, it would have guaranteed economic ruin to their masters, since little work would have been done.

(11) The world of the Southern plantation was much different than the world of the concentration camp. Slaves were not kept at starvation levels (though they were rarely satisfied with the food, clothing, and shelter provided), so slaves were not just concentrating on survival. The concentration camp was much more brutal than Southern slavery.[19]

(12) The slaves were an economic asset which guaranteed them more safety from cruelty than concentration camp inmates. While less than one per cent of inmates survived in many concentration camps, between 1830 and 1860 there was a 23 percent natural increase in Southern slave population every decade. Although slaves were frequently whipped and beaten,[20] most masters avoided floggings if they could. They used humiliation, solitary confinement, extra work, withholding passes, and other methods of discipline. There were good economic, religious, personal, and public reasons for not excessively beating slaves.

(13) Planters did not enforce rules to the letter. Absolute control was a myth. Owners recognized that slaves

[Continued on next page.]

Historian B

[Continued from previous page.]

restricted how much work they would do, and there was little masters could do about it.[21] On larger plantations, the overseer was the weak link in the control of the slaves. He had to balance the demands of the master against his own rapport with the slaves as a measure of his ability to control them. Thus, he was caught in the middle. He had no economic stake in the slaves. He tried to escape the monotony and hard work of the plantation by leaving on nights and weekends, which left slaves almost totally unsupervised.[22] This leeway in control over the slaves allowed them to develop other areas of life. Also, slaves had relationships other than master/slave in which they were the superior person—father, stronger personality, respected person on the plantation. Deferring to the owner was not the only part of their lives. The frequency of floggings shows the lack of infantilization as well as the lack of internalization of the owners' values (unlike in concentration camps).[23]

(14) Slave families were confronted with terrible obstacles to their survival as stable units. Marriages were not legal, and many slaves were promiscuous. In addition, slave women were sexually abused by white men.[24] Husbands couldn't protect their wives from sexual abuse, nor from physical abuse. The father was not really the head of the family in many ways. The master provided food, clothing, shelter, and determined how much care pregnant women and infants received. Slave mothers had to work, so their children got less care.[25] Slave families could be separated by sale at any time. Masters generally didn't want to separate them but many factors, such as death and debt, gave them no choice. Marriages that were broken by masters due to sales amounted to 32.4 percent.[26] Even slave children were sometimes beaten by white children, and nothing could be done. Children sometimes saw their parents beaten, which made them wonder who really had authority. Slave men almost universally preferred to marry slave women from other plantations to avoid watching them being abused.[27]

(15) Nevertheless, many slave families were strong and stable. Southern slavery was unique in the New World in that there was roughly a one-to-one ratio of male to female slaves (110 males to 100 females). In Latin America there was a great imbalance of the sex ratio: 19 men for each woman in some cases. The balance of the sexes in America permitted the development of the monogamous (one wife for each husband) slave family.[28] Fathers gained respect by hunting and fishing to add to their families' monotonous diet. Parents had a great deal of say over their children's behavior. They taught their children obedience, not total submission to the master. Fathers and mothers were well loved by their children.[29]

(16) Slavery in the United States was often cruel and deprived slaves of a happier life. Nevertheless, slavery was not totally dominant over the slaves. Slaves fought against the cruel and oppressive aspects of slavery and retained strong personality traits, a sense of community, and oftentimes a strong and stable family system.

[Continued on next page.]

[Continued from previous page.]

Endnotes for Historian B

1. *An Abstract of the Evidence Delivered Before a Select Committee of the House of Commons, 1790–91*, (London, 1791), pp. 39–44.
2. Daniel P. Mannix and Malcolm Crowley, *Black Cargoes: A History of the Atlantic Slave Trade, 1815–1865*, (New York, 1962), p. 111.

   There were "fairly detailed accounts of fifty-five mutinies on slavers (slave ships) from 1699 to 1845, not to mention passing references to more than a hundred others."
3. Gustavus Vassa, *The Interesting Narrative of the Life of Olandah Equiano or Gustavus Vassa, the African* (London, 1794), pp. 1–61.
4. William Wells Brown, *Narrative of William W. Brown, A Fugitive Slave* (Boston, 1847), pp. 21–30, 37–41.
5. Daniel J. Crowley, "Negro Folklore: An Africanist's View," *Texas Quarterly*, V (Autumn, 1962) pp. 65–71; John F. Szwed, "Musical Adaptation Among Afro-Americans," *Journal of American Folklore* LXXII (April–June, 1969), p. 115.
6. J. Carlyle Sitterson, "The McCollams: A Planter Family of the Old and New South," *Journal of Southern History* VI (August, 1940) pp. 347–67; H. N. McTyeire, et al. *Duties of Masters of Servants: Three Premium Essays* (Charleston, S.C., 1851), p. 136.
7. Frederick Douglass, *My Bondage and My Freedom* (New York, 1855), pp. 251–56.
8. George W. Cable, "Creole Slave Songs," *Century Magazine* XXXI (April, 1886), pp. 807–28.
9. Joel Chandler Harris, *The Complete Tales of Uncle Remus* (Boston, 1955), and Langston Hughes and Arna Bontemps, eds., *The Book of Negro Folklore* (New York, 1966).
10. Lunsford, Lane, *The Narrative of Lunsford Lane* (Boston, 1848), pp. 20–21.
11. Donald D. Wax, "Negro Resistance to the Early American Slave Trade," *Journal of Negro History*, LI (January, 1966), p. 11.
12. Douglass, pp. 91, 333, 422.
13. Herbert Aptheker, *American Negro Slave Revolts* (New York, 1943), pp. 207, 280, 336.
14. Herbert H. S. Aimes, *A History of Slavery in Cuba, 1511 to 1868* (New York, 1967) pp. 89, 160, 264.
15. William Gilmore Simms, *The Yemassee* (1832), *The Foragers* (1855), *Mellichampe* (1836).
16. Howard Braverman, "An Unusual Characterization by a Southern Ante-Bellum Writer," *Phylon* XIX (Summer, 1958), pp. 171–79.
17. David B. Davis, *The Problem of Slavery in Western Culture* (Ithaca, New York, 1966), p. 59.
18. Milton Cantor, "The Image of the Negro in Colonial Literature," *New England Quarterly* XXXVI (December, 1963), pp. 452–77.
19. John Brown, *Slave Life in Georgia* (London, 1855) p. 191; Paul de Berker, ed., *Interaction: Human Groups in Community and Institution* (Oxford, England, 1969), pp. 7–30.
20. *Ibid.*, pp. 127–36.
21. J. Carlyle Sitterson, pp. 347–67. See also "Negro Slavery in the South," *De Bow's Review*, VII (September, 1849), p. 220.
22. J. Carlyle Sitterson, "The William J. Minor Plantations: A Study in Ante-Bellum Absentee Ownership," *Journal of Southern History* IX (February, 1943), p. 63; Charles S. Sydnor, "A Slave Owner and His Overseers," *North Carolina Historical Review* XIV (January, 1937) pp. 31–38.
23. Stanley Milgrim, "Behavioral Study of Obedience," in Warren G. Bennis et al., eds., *Interpersonal Dynamics* (Homewood, Illinois, 1964), p. 110 (not a direct quote).

   The frequent use of force in interpersonal relations shows that the low person (the slave, in this case) has not fully accepted his submissive role (that is, total obedience).

[Continued on next page.]

Endnotes for Historian B

[Continued from previous page.]

24. Annie L. Burton, *Memories of Childhood's Slavery Days* (Boston, 1909), pp. 3–9.
25. Douglass, pp. 48, 51, and Booker T. Washington, *Up From Slavery* (Cambridge, 1978), p. 4.
26. "Marriage Certificates," Bureau of Refugees. Freedmen and Abandoned Lands, Record Group 105, National Archives.

SLAVE FAMILIES

(from sample counties in three states*)

	Mississippi		Tennessee		Louisiana		Totals	
	Number	Percent	Number	Percent	Number	Percent	Number	Percent
Total Unions	1,225	--	1,123	--	540	--	2,888	--
Unbroken Families	78	6.3	226	20.1	90	16.6	394	13.6
Broken Families	1,147	93.7	897	79.9	450	83.3	2,494	86.3
Broken by:								
Master	477	39.0	302	26.8	158	29.2	937	32.4
Personal Choice	145	11.9	106	9.4	58	10.7	309	10.6
Death	509	41.5	418	37.2	226	41.8	1,153	39.9
War	16	1.3	71	6.3	8	1.4	95	3.2

* Mississippi–Adams County; Tennessee–Dyer, Gibson, Wilson, and Shelby Counties; Louisiana–Concordia Parish (County)

27. John Anderson, *The Story of the Life of John Anderson, A Fugitive Slave* (London, 1863), p. 129.
    "I did not want to marry a girl belonging to my own place, because I knew I could not bear to see her ill-treated."
28. Douglass, p. 91.
29. Charles Ball, *Slavery in the United States: A Narrative of the Life and Adventures of Charles Ball* (Lewiston, Pennsylvania, 1863), p. 211.
    "Poor as the slave is, and dependent at all times upon the arbitrary will of his master, or yet more fickle caprice of the overseer, his children look up to him in his little cabin, as their protector and supporter."

[Continued on next page.]

[Continued from previous page.]

Historian C (1974)

(1) Historians have been studying the institution of slavery in the United States for many years. One of the areas of investigation has focused on the question of how bad slavery in the United States was, and more specifically, the question of what effect slavery had on the slave personally and on slaves as families.

(2) The accepted view of slavery is that it was an evil institution which deprived slaves of freedom, treated them brutally, oppressed them psychologically, and deprived them of the basic necessities of life. The first point is true; slaves were deprived of their freedom. This by itself makes slavery an evil institution. However, this interpretation will show that each of the other points is incorrect. Historians have exaggerated the negative aspects of slavery. Actually other than taking away their freedom, slavery in the United States did not have very bad effects on slaves or slave families. Generally, slaves were well-treated by their masters. Masters were interested in the well-being of their slaves, since slaves were an economic asset to them.

(3) Previous historians have been incorrect in their interpretation of slavery because they haven't looked at statistical information on the subject. This interpretation adds to a new type of history called the New Economic History and marks the beginning of a "scientifically objective" view of slavery. My view is more accurate because I have looked at more data, using computers, than other historians have studied. While previous historians looked at a few pieces of evidence, this view is based on research on literally thousands of pieces of evidence. This interpretation is a turning point in the study of slavery, and it is another step in the Cliometric Revolution—the use of computers in the study of history.

(4) Slaves in the United States had material conditions comparable to free laborers of their time in terms of food, clothing, shelter, and medical care. As a result, slaves had a relatively high life expectancy, and the slave population increased greatly without significant imports of slaves.

(5) The belief by historians that the typical slave was poorly fed is without foundation in fact. Slaves before the Civil War had a ten percent higher caloric intake than free workers in 1879,[1] ate a great variety of food other than corn and pork (which it is commonly thought they ate exclusively),[2] and received over 100 percent of the Recommended Daily Allowance (RDA) for all nutrients.[3] Slave clothing was as good as freemen's clothing. It was coarse but durable.

(6) Shelter for slaves was also as good as or better than free housing. The key to housing conditions is the number of persons per house. Since there were 5.2 slaves per house and 5.3 freemen per house, slave quarters were probably somewhat better. Comments of observers suggest that the most typical slave houses of the late antebellum period were cabins 18 by 20 feet. Therefore, the typical slave cabin of about 1850 probably had more sleeping space per person than New York City workers had in 1893.[4]

(7) Medical care for slaves in the

[Continued on next page.]

Historian C

[Continued from pervious page.]

United States was good. Sick slaves cost owners money, so owners had good reason to keep them healthy. Evidence indicates that there were midwives on plantations, as well as nurses and even hospitals on large plantations.[5] Pregnant slave women were well treated, and instructions to overseers emphasized the good health of slaves.[6]

(8) The result of these conditions of food, clothing, shelter, and medical care for slaves was a high life expectancy (how long on average a group of people lives) and fairly low infant mortality rate. While it is true that slave life expectancy was twelve percent lower than the average for white Americans, it was as high as the life expectancy in countries such as Holland and France in the same time period, and it was higher than that for urban workers in both the United States and Europe.[7] The infant mortality rate of slaves was not significantly higher than that of whites—it was 183/1,000 for slaves and 146/1,000 for whites, which is only twenty-five percent higher.[8] Another myth about slavery is that slave mothers suffocated their children. The difference in suffocation of 17/1,000 for slaves to 2/1,000 for whites is accounted for by Sudden Infant Death Syndrome (SIDS), which was not understood at the time. Blacks have a higher incidence of SIDS.[9] Also, 17/1,000 suffocations still leaves 983/1,000 infants who probably received good care from their slave mothers.

(9) Slave families in the South were stable and provided psychological stability to slaves. The belief that slave breeding, sexual exploitation, and promiscuity destroyed the slave family is a myth.

(10) Owners sometimes subsidized slave families by providing separate houses, household gifts, and cash bonuses. Although marriages were not legal, owners encouraged them by having ceremonies and recognizing them under plantation codes (which were more important than state laws). Moreover, owners relied on families for administration (passing out clothes and food), labor discipline, population increase, and rearing slave children.

(11) When slave owners had to break up slave families by selling one or more family members to another owner, slaves fought against it. This shows the strong family ties slaves had. The abolitionist view of slave families was inconsistent. The abolitionists said black families had no meaning, but they also said the breakup of the families was heart-rending.

(12) Actually, owners broke up families infrequently. Owners in the older slave states, such as Virginia, did not breed slaves for export to the new slave states, such as Mississippi, since the net profit of slave sales was equal to only one percent of gross agricultural output of the South, which is an insignificant percentage. That slave sales across state lines were infrequent is also borne out by the evidence that eighty-four percent of the slaves who moved from one state to another moved with their masters, so only sixteen percent moved through sales.[10]

[Continued on next page.]

Historian C

[Continued from previous page.]

(13) Moreover, slave sales themselves did not often break up marriage. Thirteen percent or less of interregional slave sales resulted in the destruction of marriages.[11] Since slave sales accounted for only sixteen percent of all interregional movement of slaves, the destruction of marriages by sale was only about two percent of the movement of slaves (16% of 13% = about 2%).

(14) Another statistic supports the view of the infrequency of destruction or separation of slave families by sale. The total yearly sales of slaves was only 1.92 percent of the slave population.[12] While other views of slave sales have relied on the subjective observations of first-hand witnesses, this view uses hard data, which shows that very few slaves were sold.

(15) Owners did not breed slaves for sale. This is shown by evidence that the rates of return on men and women slaves in the so-called breeding states were approximately the same. If women were being used to breed, they would have received a higher rate of return than men (since they would have been working *and* producing children). Breeding would not have done owners any good in any event, since slave women were already producing children at their biological maximum.

(16) Slave families, then, were not destroyed by slave breeding, sexual exploitation, and promiscuity. Under the careful control of plantation owners, slaves had the chance to develop stable families. In this environment, fathers developed the leadership of the family. Owners listed slave fathers as the head of the family. Evidence shows that mothers gave a great deal of care to their children. For example, mothers must have nursed their infants for twelve months because they had children more than twenty-four months apart.

(17) Slaves were not physically abused or punished. Slaves were more often given positive incentives for which they worked hard. The positive incentives included prizes for individuals or work gangs, year-end bonuses, grants of land, occasionally profit-sharing, promotion to artisan (craftsman) or driver, and the possibility of manumission (freedom).[13] Slaves had other opportunities to better themselves, as well. The common belief that all slaves were menial laborers is false. Over twenty-five percent of males were managers, professionals, craftsmen, and semiskilled workers.[14]

(18) Force was an important aspect in getting slaves to work hard. The judicious use of force could get the desired result at less cost to the owner, which is similar to parental use of force. However, the system of positive incentives, not force, was the principal basis of promoting the work of slaves. The notion that the slave owners relied on the whip alone to promote discipline and efficiency is a highly misleading myth. Whipping was the most common form of discipline, but there were many others. Barrow plantation records show 0.7 whippings per slave per year, which is certainly a low total.[15] Besides, whipping is not unusual through history; we see it in the Bible and many other places.

(19) Slaves were taken care of by their

[Continued on next page.]

Historian C

[Continued from previous page.]

masters in many ways. In exchange, the masters expropriated (took away) twelve percent of the slaves' labor output. This is much lower than the approximately thirty-percent tax rate charged for government services today. Slaves got a type of welfare from owners at a cheap cost.

(20) As a result of the positive incentive system, slaves identified with their masters. Slave rebellions were rare because of the opportunities within slavery. Slaves also worked very hard. Slave workers were just as or more efficient than white free workers. Plantations had greater output per worker per year than Northern farms.[16] This was due to more extensive specialization, better management techniques, and better control on plantations. Historians who see slave workers as lazy and inefficient base their theory on the observations of Frederick Olmstead who visited the South before the Civil War. The problem is that he was in the South in the slack season, when less work was done, so his conclusions are based on an unrepresentative sample. How could nationally known, intelligent planters have profited from poor workers? Historians who see slaves as inefficient are racists.

(21) Certainly slavery was bad in that it deprived people of liberty. Otherwise, however, historians have exaggerated its negative aspects. Overall, slaves were well cared for in terms of food, clothing, shelter, and medical care; their families were not ruined by slavery; and they were not excessively abused by owners. The plantation was a highly efficient economic unit in which black slave workers and white plantation managers worked hard and cooperated to make the greatest profit. After slaves were emancipated their situation worsened considerably—they received lower wages, had poorer health, had a lower life expectancy, and had fewer skills. Blacks had been materially better off under slavery.

Endnotes for Historian C

1. U.S. Census Office, 8th Census, 1860, *Agriculture of the United States in 1860*, Washington, GPO, 1860. (See table at top of next page.)

   The fallacy in the position of those who argue that slaves were poorly fed stems from the failure to recognize the implications of the fact that the South in general, and big plantations in particular, produced large quantities of food in addition to pork and corn. If these other foods were not being consumed by slaves, where were they going?

2. More careful reading of plantation documents shows that the slave diet included many foods in addition to corn and pork. Among plantation products which slaves consumed were beef, mutton, chickens, milk, turnips, peas, squashes, sweet potatoes, apples, plums, oranges, pumpkins, and peaches...salt, sugar, and molasses...fish, coffee, and whiskey.

[Continued on next page.]

Endnotes for Historian C

[Continued from previous page.]

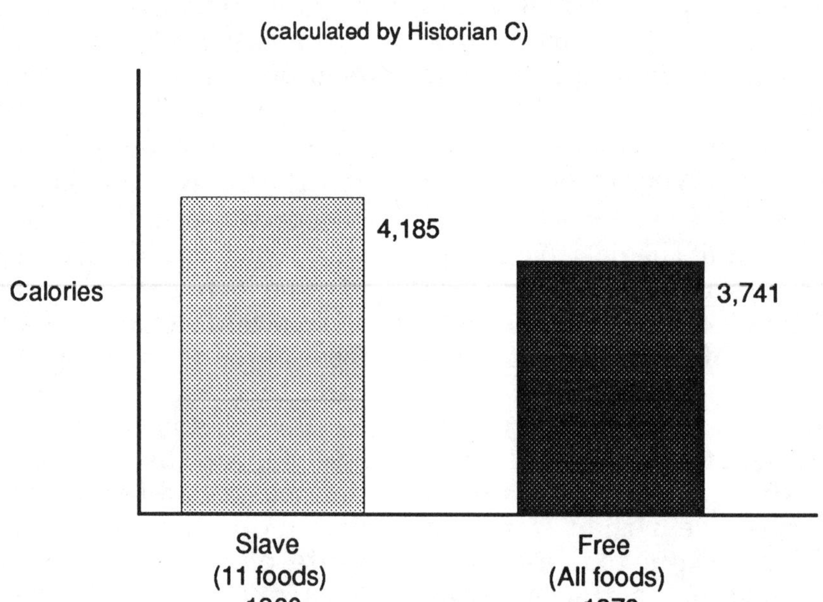

3. The Nutritional Value of the Slave Diet: Average Slave Consumption of Various Nutrients in 1869 as a Percentage of Modern Recommended Daily Allowances (calculated by Historian C): 100 percent is the amount recommended of each nutrient per day.

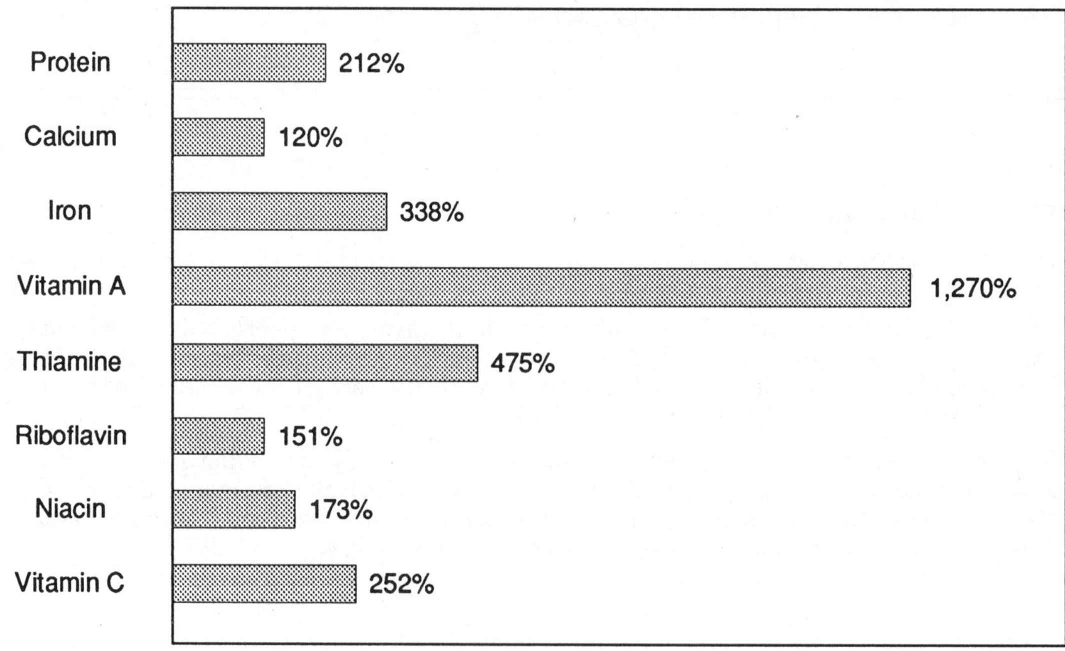

[Continued on next page.]

Endnotes for Historian C

[Continued from previous page.]

4. U.S. Bureau of Labor Special Report, *The Slums of Baltimore, Chicago, New York, and Philadelphia*, 1894, pp. 12, 23, 24.
5. On one plantation with 168 slaves, for example, the hospital was a two-story brick building which had eight large rooms.
6. Record of instructions of slave owner J. A. S. Acklen to his overseer:

   "The preservation of the health of the negroes, and the care of them when sick, will require your best attention."

   Record of instructions by slave owner C. P. Weston to his overseer:

   "Your first object is to be, under all circumstances, the care and well being of the negroes."
7. Robert Evans, Jr., "The Economics of American Negro Slavery," in Universities National Bureau Committee for Economic Research, *Aspects of Labor Economics*, Princeton: Princeton University Press, 1962, Table 16, p. 212.

   Evans estimates the male life expectancy of slaves at 36 years.

THE LIFE EXPECTATION AT BIRTH FOR U.S. SLAVES AND VARIOUS FREE POPULATIONS, 1830–1920

Place and Period	Years
U.S., white, 1850	40
England and Wales, 1839–54	40
Holland, 1850–59	36
France, 1854–58	36
U.S., slave, 1850	**36**
Italy, 1885	35
Austria, 1875	31
Chile, 1920	31
Manchester, England, 1850	24
New York, Boston, and Philadelphia, 1830	24

[Continued on next page.]

Endnotes for Historian C

[Continued from previous page.]

8. Of every thousand slaves born in 1850, an average 183 died before their first birthday. The death rate for white infants in the same year was 146 per thousand. In other words, the infant death rate for slaves was 25 percent higher than for whites....Most of the difference between the infant death rates of slaves and free persons appears to have been due to the fact that the South was a less healthy environment than the North. The infant death rate of southern whites in 1850 was 177 per thousand—virtually the same as the infant death rate for slaves. Death rate of 183/1,000 for slave infants is from Evans (see endnote 7).
9. Abraham B. Bergman and J. Bruce Beckwith, "Sudden Death Syndrome in Infancy," in Morris Green and Robert J. Haggerty, eds., *Ambulatory Pediatrics*, Philadelphia: W. B. Saunders, 1968, pp. 777–78.
10. The figure of 84 percent was arrived at by dividing William Calderhead's estimates of the number of slaves sold from Maryland between 1830 and 1860 by Claudia Goldin's estimates of the net migration out of Maryland between 1830 and 1860.

    William Calderhead, "How Extensive Was the Border State Slave Trade? A New Look," *Civil War History*, Vol. XVIII (March, 1972), pp. 42–55.
11. Figures taken from New Orleans slave sale invoices.

    We consider as slave marriages all unions that the slaves involved intended, or expected, to be "stable," regardless of what view others may have had of these unions. For the purposes of the breakup rate, we take as evidence of such intent the existence of a child. In other words, we consider every case of a slave woman who is sold with a child but without a husband to be a broken marriage.
12. A study of slave trading in Maryland over the decade from 1830 to 1840 revealed that total sales (local and interstate) amounted to 1.92 percent of the population each year.

    The 1.92 percent figure is based upon Anne Arundel County, Maryland, since this is the county with the most complete data. Historian C checked with Calderhead (see footnote 10 for citation) and got total sales from records at holdings and estates.
13. Analysis of occupational data derived from probate and plantation records reveals an unusual distribution of ages among slave artisans. Slaves in their twenties were substantially underrepresented, while slaves in their forties and fifties were overrepresented. This age pattern suggests that the selection of slaves for training in the crafts was frequently delayed until slaves reached their late twenties, or perhaps even into their thirties....

    He (the slave owner) could, therefore, treat entry into the skilled occupations as a prize that was to be claimed by the most deserving, regardless of family background....Extra effort (was) put forth by young field hands who competed for these jobs.
14. From the Parker-Gallman sample of records from U.S. Census, 1860, *Agriculture of the United States in 1860*. The sample was taken from parishes (counties) in Louisiana.

    Within the agricultural sector, about 7.0 percent of the men held managerial posts and 11.9 percent were skilled craftsmen (blacksmiths, carpenters, coopers, etc.). Another 7.4 percent were engaged in semiskilled and domestic or quasi-domestic jobs: teamsters, coachmen, gardeners, stewards, and house servants.

    The share of skilled and semiskilled laborers in nonfield occupations on plantations was determined from a sample of 33 estates, ranging in size from 3 to 98 slaves. The information was retrieved from probate records.

    On large slaveholdings (over 50 slaves) only one out of every four owners used white overseers....

    Only 30 percent of plantations with one hundred or more slaves employed white overseers. On smaller plantations the proportion was even lower....

    The conclusion indicated by these findings is startling: On a majority of the large plantations, the top nonownership management was black.

[Continued on next page.]

Endnotes for Historian C

[Continued from previous page.]

15. Diary of Bennet H. Barrow

    Reliable data on the frequency of whipping is extremely sparse. The only systematic record of whipping now available for an extended period comes from the diary of Bennet Barrow, a Louisiana planter who believed that to spare the rod was to spoil the slave. His plantation numbered about 200 slaves, of whom about 120 were in the labor force. The record shows that over the course of two years a total of 160 whippings were administered, an average of 0.7 whippings per hand per year. About half the hands were not whipped during the period.

    The table below lists the distribution of whippings on the Bennet H. Barrow Plantation during a two-year period beginning in December, 1840.

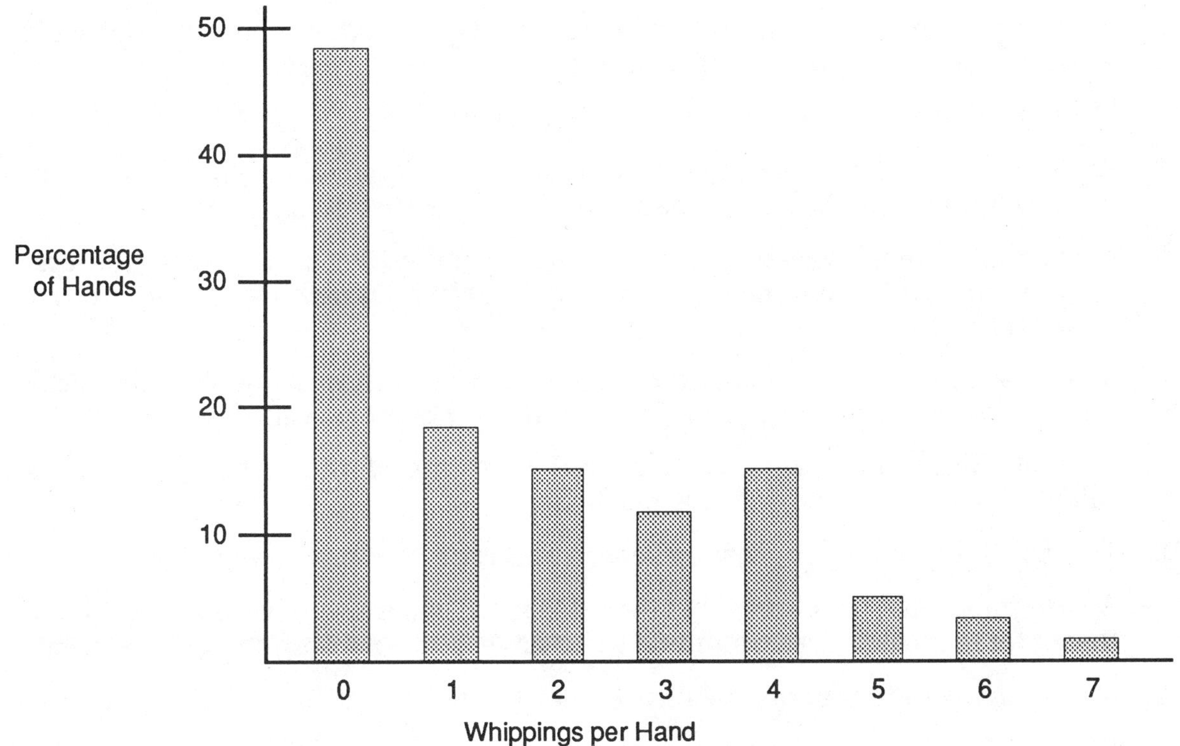

16. Southern agriculture as a whole was about 35 percent more efficient than Northern agriculture in 1860....Southern slave farms were 28 percent more efficient than Southern free farms.

[Continued on next page.]

[Continued from previous page.]

Relevant Information

1. The slave population in the United States increased by reproduction. That is, on average more slaves were born than died each year. In other slave societies in the Western Hemisphere (for example, in Cuba, Haiti, and Jamaica) slaves did not live long enough to replace themselves. The slaves had to be replaced by the slave trade from Africa.
2. Concentration camps were set up by the German Nazi Party under Adolf Hitler. The main purpose of concentration camps was to kill people. Eventually concentration camps were used to accomplish Hitler's "final solution," the extermination (killing) of all Jews in Europe.
3. In concentration camps people were herded into large barracks with very unsanitary conditions. The guards were not concerned if people died of diseases (as long as the guards didn't get the diseases).
4. Torture and brutality were a regular feature of concentration camps. Often it was arbitrary—people were picked at random to be tortured.
5. Millions of people died in concentration camps.
6. Whether or not slave marriages were regarded as legal, slaves lived in family units. That is, a husband, wife, and children lived together.
7. Many slaves were house servants, nannies, or skilled workers (i.e., carpenters, coopers, etc.), although most slaves were field hands, picking cotton or other plantation crops.
8. Most slaves lived on farms and plantations of less than 20 slaves. On these farms, slaves worked with and often knew their owners well.
9. The efficiency of workers is measured in terms of productivity, which is calculated as output per worker per hour.
10. The South has a longer growing season than the North.
11. A whipping could be a brutal beating although owners were cautious not to go too far for fear of killing or maiming their slaves, thus ruining their investment.
12. Many slaves were married to slaves on different plantations.
13. Washington, D.C. and Baltimore, Maryland were major slave trading centers. Slave sales here would have been recorded on the Washington, D.C. and Baltimore registries, not on local county records.
14. Anne Arundel county is near Washington, D.C. and Baltimore.
15. Louisiana produced mostly sugar, not cotton.
16. Sugar production requires barrel makers (coopers) while cotton does not. Thus, sugar production may require more skilled workers than does cotton.

[Continued on next page.]

Relevant Information

[Continued from previous page.]

17. Although treatment varied from country to country and region to region, on a whole, slaves in Latin America were treated as poorly as in the United States. In fact, on many Caribbean Islands, such as Cuba, the life expectancies of slaves was much lower than in the United States. That is, slaves lived much longer in the United States.
18. The New Orleans sales invoices do not describe the prior marital status of women or men in the New Orleans slave market. The only demographic data indicated for all slaves sold are age and sex.

Comments on the Books (from the book jackets)

Historian A

1. "This book is bold and original. It fearlessly employs the methods and materials of history, economics, anthropology, and social psychology."
   —John Hope Franklin, *Massachusetts Review*
2. "There is no other word for this book but brilliant."
   —Louis Filler, *The Ohio Historical Quarterly*
3. "[The author] has now demonstrated how old and well-worked subjects can become excitingly new...a book of capital importance."
   —*The Virginia Quarterly Review*
4. "Probably the most useful single book on slavery to appear in fifty years."
   —*British Journal of Sociology*

Historian B

1. "Doubly welcome, both for its intrinsic worth in describing slavery as it must have been for those 'inside' and for its meaning for scholarship...based largely on the autobiographies of fugitive slaves and survivors of slavery, [this book] shatters the notion that slaves were molded by a common experience into a common mold of shuffling subserviency...a book all American historians could read with profit."
   —Willie Lee Rose, the Johns Hopkins University, in *The Journal of American History*

[Continued on next page.]

[Continued from previous page.]

2. "This is the volume on American slavery that students are soon likely to find as required reading...[The author] has done more than anyone else to penetrate the life and mind of the slave community...."

   —Walter B. Weare, University of Wisconsin, in *Civil War History*

3. "A sober and sane treatment of an aspect of Negro slavery which has usually been neglected and distorted."

   —Kenneth Wiggins Porter, Arizona State University, in *The Journal of Southern History*

Historian C

1. "If a more important book about American history has been published in the last decade, I don't know about it. [This book] is at once a jarring attack on the methods and conclusions of traditional scholarship and a lucid, highly readable analysis of the special American problem—black slavery. It isn't going to make anyone with an established interest in the subject very happy, but then, that's the point....[The authors] have with one stroke turned around a whole field of interpretation and exposed the frailty of history done without science."

   —Peter Passell, *New York Times Book Review*

2. "When I first heard of [this book], my reaction to it was: 'Even is it's true, I won't believe it.' Now that I have read the text, I am convinced and ready to believe it."

   —Louis Gottschall

3. "Detailed, absorbing, and exceedingly controversial. I wouldn't think that any person who pretends to knowledge of the time and region could possibly ignore it."

   —John Kenneth Galbraith

4. "[The authors'] startling conclusions are bound to provoke continuing controversy...[the book] is certain to influence discussions of slavery for a long time to come."

   —David Brion Davis

5. "It is absolutely stunning, quite simply the most exciting and provocative book I've read in years....It will stand out as a remarkable achievement."

   —Stephen Albert Thernstrom

[Continued on next page.]

Worksheet: Historians on Slavery

Historian A

1. What is the main point of Historian A's argument?

2. In paragraph 2, Historian A uses a type of reasoning which he then tries to prove in the next three paragraphs. List below the type of reasoning and evaluate it. (Remember, the question to ask for each type of reasoning can be found in Unit 1, "Guide to Critical Thinking.")

   Type of Reasoning:

   Key Question:

   Evaluation:

3. What is the type of reasoning that is primarily used in paragraph 12? Evaluate it.

4. In paragraph 8, Historian A says that since there is no evidence of the passive personality in Latin America, the passive personality must not have existed. What is the possible fallacy here? (Refer to Unit 1, "Guide to Critical Thinking," pp. 12–13.)

[Continued on next page.]

[Continued from previous page.]

5. A point which is crucial to Historian A's argument is the existence of the passive personality among slaves in the United States (paragraph 7). If he can show that a high percentage of slaves were passive, then he has support for the argument that slave personalities were crushed by slavery. If he cannot show that the passive personality was common, then many of his other points collapse as well. How well does Historian A establish the existence of the passive personality?

6. Evaluate one piece of evidence for Historian A.

7. Overall, how strong is Historian A's evidence?

Q Historian B

8. What is the main point of Historian B?

_______9. How does Historian B's argument compare with Historian A's argument?

A. He tries to back up Historian A's argument.

B. He supports most of Historian A's argument.

C. He doesn't support or attack Historian A's argument.

D. He attacks one or two of Historian A's minor points.

E. He attacks Historian A's basic argument.

[Continued on next page.]

[Continued from previous page.]

10. Put a check on the line next to each statement from Historian B which supports the argument that slaves had minds of their own, rather than infantile, passive personalities.

______A. Slaves had their own recreation and religion.

______B. Slaves frequently ran away.

______C. Slaves were frequently whipped.

______D. There were fewer slave revolts in the United States than in Latin America.

11. In paragraph 8, Historian B tries to show that the reason there were fewer slave revolts in the United States was not due to more passive personalities among United States slaves. How well does he prove this point?

12. In paragraph 14, Historian B says, "Marriages that were broken by masters due to sales amounted to 32.4 percent."[26] List below the main type of reasoning used, and evaluate it. You can better figure out the type of reasoning by looking at endnote 26.

Type of Reasoning:

Key Question:

Evaluation:

13. Are most of Historian B's sources primary or secondary? Explain.

[Continued on next page.]

[Continued from previous page.]

14. Evaluate the evidence in the following:
    A. Endnote 2

    B. Endnote 29

Historian C

15. What is the main point of Historian C?

_____16. What type of reasoning does Historian C use in paragraph 2?
  A. Comparison (analogy)
  B. Generalization
  C. Cause and Effect
  D. Proof
  E. Debating

17. In paragraph 3
    A. What type of reasoning is the first sentence ("Previous historians...")?

[Continued on next page.]

[Continued from previous page.]

B. What is possibly wrong with the second sentence ("This interpretation...")?

C. What is the possible fallacy in the third and fourth sentences ("My view...")? (Hint: Look under proof fallacies in Unit 1, "Guide to Critical Thinking," pp. 12–13.)

18. Assume the evidence for paragraph 7 is true and accurate. What is nevertheless a possible problem with the argument? (Hint: It has to do with the type of reasoning used.)

19. In paragraph 12, Historian C argues that most slaves (84%) were not sold but rather were moved with their owners. Thus, he concludes, most slave families were not broken by being moved. What is an important assumption which Historian C makes here? (Hint: Look at the relevant information.)

20. In endnote 12, Historian C uses Anne Arundel County, Maryland, to show that slave families in the South before the Civil War were not frequently destroyed (separated) by sale. What might be wrong with this reasoning?

[Continued on next page.]

[Continued from previous page.]

21. Look at the relevant information. According to this information, what is wrong with Anne Arundel County as a sample of slave sales throughout the South?

22. In paragraph 17, Historian C says, "The common belief that all slaves were menial laborers is false." List below the primary type of reasoning used and evaluate it.

    Type of Reasoning:

    Key Question:

    Evaluation:

23. Endnote 14 supports the argument that many slaves were more than menial laborers. What is a possible weakness in this evidence?

24. In paragraph 18, Historian C argues that slaves were not whipped very often by showing that on the Barrow Plantation, there were only 0.7 whippings per slave per year. What is possibly wrong with this argument?

[Continued on next page.]

[Continued from previous page.]

25. In paragraph 20, the author argues that slaves were just as, or more efficient than, Northern free white workers. List below the main type of reasoning used and evaluate it.

    Type of Reasoning:

    Key Question:

    Evaluation:

26. In the last sentence in paragraph 20, what is the possible fallacy? (Use your "Guide to Critical Thinking," pp. 12–14.)

Overall

27. Which of the three viewpoints is strongest, and why?

LESSON 17 What Do Visual Sources Show about Slavery?

One way to get a better sense of what slavery was like in the United States is to gather evidence about it. Certainly the testimony of slaves, owners, and observers are important, along with plantation and census records. But a different kind of evidence than the printed word can be obtained from visual sources. Like all other sources, they must be evaluated for their reliability.

Examine the visual sources that follow, then fill in the chart (p. 135) and answer the questions. Be careful in your evaluation of the reliability of each source. Look at the information under each visual source in making your evaluation.

As part of your evaluation, note the type of medium used to create the picture: drawing, painting, lithograph, engraving, or photograph. A lithograph is a type of printing done by drawing the picture on a flat stone, then transferring the image to paper using ink. A wood engraving is done by carving the picture into wood, then copying to paper using ink.

Source A

Library of Congress photoduplication no. LC-USZ62-23797

"The Old Plantation Home"
Lithograph by Currier and Ives, 1872
Currier and Ives was a large company. The name of the artist is not given.
The caption says, "A rural scene. Eight blacks of all ages have gathered to dance."

[Continued on next page.]

[Continued from previous page.]

Source B

Library of Congress photoduplication no. LC-USZ62-2582

"A Slave Auction at the South"
Wood engraving from a sketch by T. R. Davis
The engraving appeared in *Harpers Weekly*, Volume V, July 13, 1861, p. 442.

[Continued on next page.]

[Continued from previous page.]

Source C

Library of Congress photoduplication no. LC-USZ62-345

"A Cotton Plantation on the Mississippi"
Chromolithograph by Currier and Ives, 1884
William Aiken Walker painted the scene from which the chromolithograph was made.
Mr. Walker did many paintings in the 1880s of plantations and the New Orleans levee.

[Continued on next page.]

[Continued from previous page.]

Source D

Library of Congress photoduplication no. LC-USZ62-12848

"Southern Cotton Plantation and Southern Negro Quarters"
Lithograph by Goes Litho Co., 1897

[Continued on next page.]

[Continued from previous page.]

Source E

National Archives photo no. W&C 109

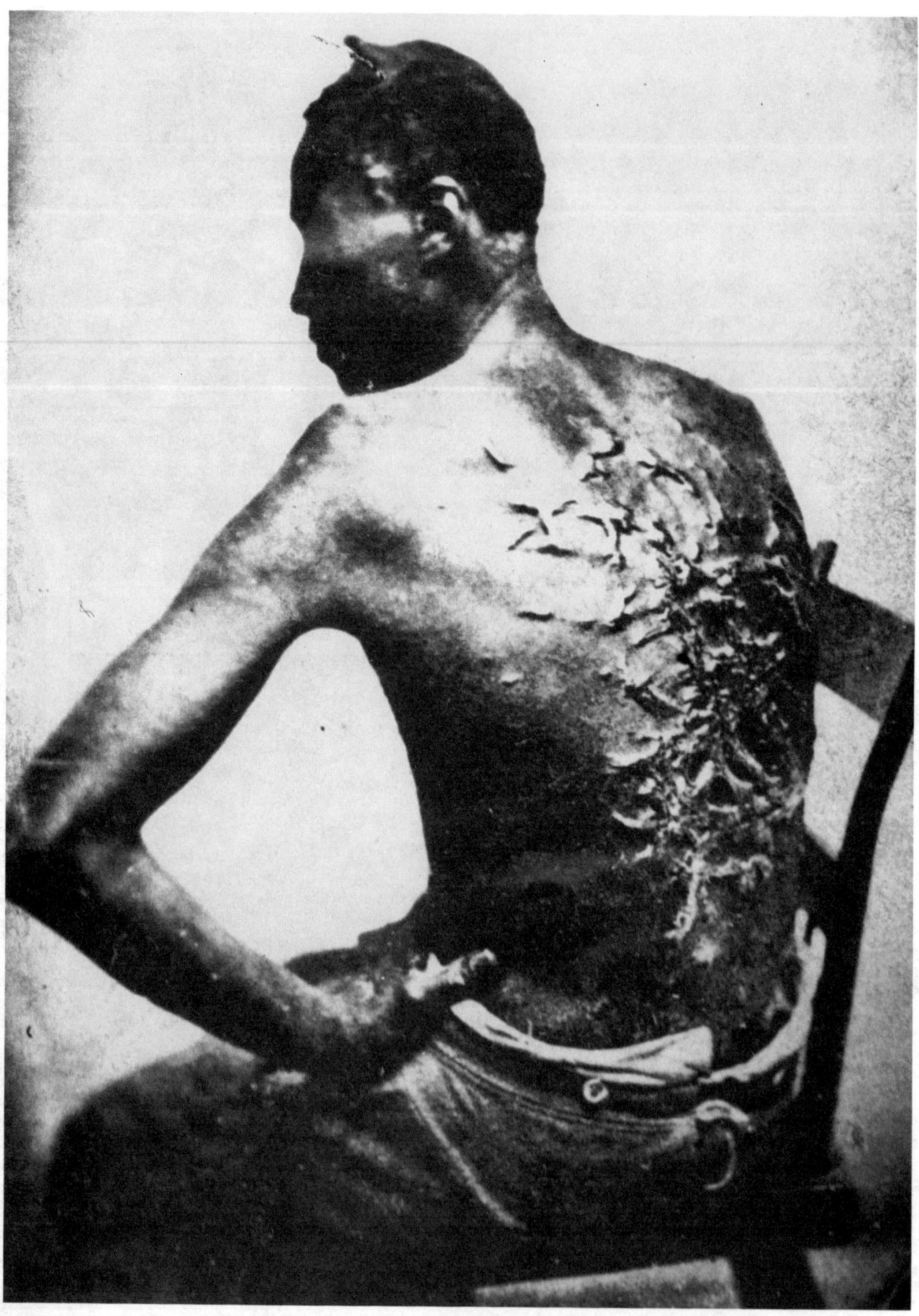

Untitled. Photograph taken at Baton Rogue, Louisiana, April 2, 1863, in the War Department Files, National Archives. This information appears with the photograph: "Overseer Artayou Carrier whipped me. I was two months in bed sore from the whipping. My master came after I was whipped; he discharged [fired] the overseer. The very words of poor Peter, taken as he sat for his picture."

[Continued on next page.]

[Continued from previous page.]

Source F

Library of Congress photoduplication no. LC-USZ62-8338

"Cotton Plantation, Mississippi"

Photograph of painting. Copyright, March 19, 1906. No artist name on painting or photograph. Copyrights are generally submitted soon after the products are done.

[Continued on next page.]

[Continued from previous page.]

Source G

Library of Congress photoduplication no. LC-USZ62-30849

Group of Negroes singing while shucking corn on plantation; chorus—"Sing, Darkeys, Sing."
Woodcut by Whitney and Annin from a sketch by the popular artist Felix Darley (1822–1888) for the book
Uncle Tom's Cabin Contrasted with Buckingham Hall, the Planter's Home, by Robert Criswell, New York: D. Sanshaw, 1852, p. 65.

[Continued on next page.]

[Continued from previous page.]

Source	What type of visual source is it?	What does it show about slavery?	How reliable is this source? (Consider at least 2 criteria.)
A			
B			
C			
D			
E			
F			
G			

[Continued on next page.]

[Continued from previous page.]

Questions

1. Overall, what do the sources show about slavery?

2. Which source is most reliable and which source is least reliable? Why?

3. Look at the pictures of slavery in your textbook. What impressions do they give you about slavery?

LESSON 18 Were Slaves Fed an Adequate Diet?

In this lesson you'll be focusing on two questions: Were slaves fed enough calories? and Were slaves fed a nutritious diet? You'll be reading a series of historical viewpoints on these two questions. The viewpoints should convey the variety of approaches that historians use to examine a subject, and it should illustrate how interpretations change over time. Pay attention to the relevant information and the dates of the interpretations in parentheses.

Relevant Information

1. Slavery in the United States lasted from about 1670 to 1865.
2. There were millions of slaves in the United States over this time period (four million in 1860 alone). Slaves were in Southern states only.
3. The highest population of slaves in the United States worked on cotton plantations, but many others worked on tobacco, sugar, and indigo plantations, and still others worked in other occupations.
4. Slaves had a wide variety of tasks on United States plantations and lived significantly differently from one another.
5. Blacks have different nutritional characteristics than whites:
    a. Blacks suffer from sickle cell anemia. This disorder makes them have a higher iron and folic acid requirement.
    b. Black pigmentation reduces the absorption of vitamin D from the sun, thus increasing the amount required from diet.
    c. Lactose intolerance causes blacks to get sick when they drink animal milk. Without drinking animal milk, it would be very difficult at that time to get enough calcium.
6. A deficiency of calcium and vitamin D would make it difficult for blacks to absorb other nutrients.
7. Vitamin D is absorbed from the sun. It is highly unlikely to get enough from food. (That's why they fortify milk with vitamin D today.)
8. It is unusual not to get enough magnesium from food. Alcoholics sometimes suffer from magnesium deficiency (DTs) because they eat little food. One meal per day is enough to prevent it.
9. The slave population in the United States increased by reproduction. That is, slaves lived long enough to cause the slave population to increase.
10. Potassium is readily available in a wide variety of foods. It is difficult not to get enough. It also is easily lost through diarrhea or vomiting.

[Continued on next page.]

Relevant Information

[Continued from previous page.]

11. Calcium is available in dairy products, leafy green vegetables, and molasses.
12. The main source of iron is red meat (beef, etc.). The pork slaves ate, however, was probably mostly fat, not meat, so it was lower in iron. Molasses is high in iron.
13. Slaves ate a lot of corn, pork, and molasses.
14. A deficiency in vitamin D results in rickets or tetany in children.
15. A deficiency in thiamine can result in edema or beriberi.

Viewpoint I. Historians A (1918), B (1924), C (1936), D (1956)

Adult-slave field hands were issued a standard ration of 3 1/2 pounds of salt pork and 1 peck (about 8 quarts or 4 liters) of corn meal per week. These historians conclude that this is a monotonous diet which would cause deficiencies in vitamins and minerals, despite the fact it would be high in calories.

Viewpoint II. Historian E (Hypothetical)

Slaves were well fed as evidenced by their hard work. You can't do all that work without having eaten a lot of food for energy. Historians A, B, C, D are wrong in saying that slaves were poorly fed.

Viewpoint III. Historians F and G (1974)

Historians who feel slaves were poorly fed are wrong. Slaves were adequately fed in both calories and nutrients. Historians who feel that slaves were fed only pork and corn base their views on instructions by some masters to their overseers. They overlook the fact, however, that plantation documents mention many other foods besides pork and corn; for example, beef, mutton, chickens, milk, turnips, peas, squashes, sweet potatoes, apples, plums, oranges, pumpkins, peaches, salt, sugar, coffee, molasses, fish, and whiskey.

Looking at the plantation from a different perspective gives a different view of the slave diet. By taking the livestock inventories and crop yields from the 1860 census, we can use conversion tables to find out the meat and food productions. We then subtract out a small percentage of food consumed by whites (whites formed less than ten percent of the population of the plantations we sampled), a small percentage fed to animals (since mainly corn was fed to animals), and a small percentage of beef and pork which would be sold off the plantation. What is left is what was consumed by slaves. What other historians have failed to ask themselves is, If these other foods were not being consumed by slaves, where were they going? By this estimate, we get these percentages of energy derived by slaves from foods:

[Continued on next page.]

Viewpoint III

[Continued from previous page.]

Food	Percent of Energy		Calories
Pork	13.0	Subtotal 67.1	543
Corn	54.1		2,265
Cowpeas	10.2	Subtotal 32.9	427
Sweet Potatoes	10.1		424
Other food	12.6		526
Totals	100.0		4,185

It is obvious from this analysis that slaves enjoyed a more varied diet than just corn and pork.

From the number of calories consumed per day, we calculate that slaves had the following percentages of Recommended Daily Allowances:

Nutrient	Percent of RDA
Protein	212
Calcium	120
Iron	338
Vitamin A	1,270
Riboflavin	151
Niacin	173
Vitamin C	252

So slaves exceeded the RDA of all the major nutrients.

[Continued on next page.]

[Continued from previous page.]

Viewpoint IV. Historian H (1975)

Historians F and G are wrong in their interpretations that slaves were well fed.

First, they claim that there were many foods mentioned in plantation documents. No doubt they were mentioned somewhere at some time in the South. This doesn't prove the slaves ate these foods frequently or even occasionally. Just because one plantation in Virginia mentioned turnips in its records from 1820 doesn't prove that slaves regularly ate turnips.

Second, Historians F and G incorrectly estimate the residue (what is left over) of food for slaves to eat. They convert livestock inventories and crop yields to food output by using conversion tables. But the conversion tables are from 1900, not 1860. In 1900 the commercial food processing industry had arisen and better techniques were used in converting crops and meat to food. The result is that they have *under*estimated the quantity of pork and corn produced and *over*estimated the quantities of meats, grains, and milk.

Third, the sample of plantations that Historians F and G use to derive the residue of food consumed by slaves is weak. It is only for plantations with more than 50 slaves which were 50 miles or more from a city. Slaves were probably better fed on larger plantations.

Fourth, Historians F and G underestimated the amount of food besides corn that was fed to animals. For example, five responses to a United States Patent Office questionnaire in 1849 show that cowpeas were fed to hogs and cattle, and used as fertilizer.

By using Historian F and G's figures but correcting for their mistakes, one gets the following results:

Food	Percent of Energy		Calories
Pork	16.3	Subtotal 82.9	685
Corn	66.6		2,803
Cowpeas	3.5	Subtotal 17.1	149
Sweet Potatoes	5.5		233
Other food	8.0		336
Totals	100.0		4,206

[Continued on next page.]

Viewpoint IV

[Continued from previous page.]

One can see that, as historians have concluded for years, slaves were fed a monotonous diet of corn and pork, and very little other foods. The high number of calories certainly exceeds what is consumed today, but was not excessive for the work slaves had to do. In fact, it would appear that 4,206 calories would be enough for a *lightly* to *moderately* worked slave. If a slave were worked harder than this, he would begin to suffer. It would seem that the slave diet was not generous, but simply allowed a person to work like a slave.

Viewpoint V. Historians F and G (1975)

Historian H has criticized our thesis that slaves were adequately fed. This criticism is only on the nutritional adequacy of the slave diet, however, for Historian H accepts the high calorie content that we proposed.

We believe that there are many errors in Historian H's argument, but we will begin by accepting his revisions.

One interesting point is that Historian H's revised diet for slaves would have cost slave owners seven cents more per slave per day. He does not address this question: Why did slave owners prefer a narrow diet, lacking in variety, when they could have simultaneously increased variety and reduced cost without any loss in energy value?

Historian H also does not show the nutritive value resulting from his revised diet. The values exceed the Recommended Daily Allowances of protein, calcium, iron, vitamin A, thiamine, niacin, and vitamin C. Only riboflavin is below recommended levels, although it is still well above minimum levels (Minimum Daily Requirements).

One should not accept Historian H's diet, however. He assumes that slave foods were limited to the ten foods he has listed. True, we also limited our analysis to ten foods, but this is because we wanted to prove that even this limited diet shows that slaves had a nutritionally adequate diet. Recent data has been gained from the Federal Writer's Project of the WPA. (This project from the 1930s interviewed old people who had been slaves before 1865. So most of the people were eighty-years old or older.) The nearly 2,000 WPA interviews show that slaves ate, to a significant extent, many other foods than those allotted to them by their owners, including fish, game, chicken, molasses, and many vegetables. These other foods add to the nutrient intake of slaves and lend further evidence to the contention that slaves achieved a nutritionally adequate diet.

There are many other defects in Historian H's argument, but this discussion will suffice to show that he has done little to weaken our argument.

[Continued on next page.]

[Continued from previous page.]

Viewpoint VI. Historians I and J (1977)

Other historians have looked at how much food slaves probably ate to evaluate the nutritional adequacy of the slave diet. Another approach, however, is to look at slave illnesses related to nutritional deficiencies. If slaves suffered nutritional diseases then we can conclude that they were poorly fed in terms of nutrients. We studied diseases in slave children and found that many of the diseases were related to diet, such as tetany (muscle spasms, advanced rickets), dental caries (cavities), rickets (deformed bones), edema (retaining fluid), convulsions, suffocation, pica (dirt or clay eating), worms, and others. Many diseases suffered by slave children were diagnosed as some other disease when they may have been tetany (a nutritional disease), which has symptoms in common with other diseases.

Pica, or clay eating, a practice prevalent among slaves, has several possible causes. One theory is that it is sociological. Our view is that it is caused by a deficiency of calcium, magnesium, potassium, and iron. The dirt eaten by the slaves is rich in these minerals, and patients treated with these minerals stop eating dirt.

Overall, slaves were deficient in four nutrients: calcium, magnesium, vitamin D, and iron. The deficiencies caused nutritional diseases among slaves.

Viewpoint VII. Historians K, L, M (1980)

Our study of the slave diet in Georgia and Florida from 1800 to 1860 leads us to the conclusion that slaves were able to supplement their allotment of corn and pork to achieve a nutritional diet. The typical diet of an adult male slave was 5,510 calories per day, and intake of all the major vitamins and minerals (protein, calcium, potassium, iron, thiamine, niacin, riboflavin, vitamin A, and vitamin C) exceeded the Recommended Daily Allowance by a minimum of 200 percent. The diet for a *prime hand*, one who did the most strenuous tasks, was 6,306 calories per day.

We used data from a variety of sources in our study: plantation records and documents, journals of the period, government documents on climate and production, manuals on slave care, plantation archeological reports, and zooarcheological reports.

[Continued on next page.]

[Continued from previous page.]

Worksheet

1. What is the strength of the interpretation in Viewpoint I?

2. What is wrong with Historian E's criticism in Viewpoint II? (Hint: Reread Viewpoint I. Watch the language used in Viewpoint I and Viewpoint II.)

3. Evaluate the argument in the first paragraph of Viewpoint III.

4. What type of reasoning is used in the second paragraph onward in Viewpoint III? (Hint: cause and effect, generalization, proof by eliminating alternatives, or proof by authority.) Evaluate the argument.

[Continued on next page.]

[Continued from previous page.]

5. How significant are Historian H's four criticisms of Historian F and G's interpretations in Viewpoint III?

6. Evaluate Historian F and G's defense of their interpretation in Viewpoint IV against the criticisms by Historian H.

7. Identify the type of reasoning used by Historians I and J in Viewpoint VI and evaluate it. Be sure to look back at the relevant information in assessing this argument.

8. Evaluate the generalization made in Viewpoint VII compared to the generalizations made by the other historians.

[Continued on next page.]

[Continued from previous page.]

9. What is your view of how well slaves were fed in terms of calories?

10. What is your view of how well slaves were fed in terms of nutrients? Are you more certain of your conclusion in question 9 or in this question?

11. What skills or knowledge did these historians need to study this topic?

12. Why do you think some historians worked in groups (e.g., F and G; I and J; K, L, and M)?

13. On this topic of the slave diet, are we getting closer to or further from the truth? Explain your answer.

14. What are the standards of excellence in history, and how are they "enforced"?

UNIT 4
Civil War

LESSON 19 Assessing the Reliability of Sources

Evaluate the following pieces of evidence by listing their strengths and weaknesses. If you need help, refer to the section on **Evidence** in the "Guide to Critical Thinking" (Unit 1).

1. We want to know what slavery was like in the 1850s in the South. The 1852 novel, *Uncle Tom's Cabin,* written by Harriet Beecher Stowe, showed slavery, under the brutal hand of Simon Legree, as an evil institution.

   STRENGTHS WEAKNESSES

2. We are trying to determine if Abraham Lincoln was a great statesman who tried to avoid war. In the Lincoln-Douglas debates of 1858, we find that Senator Douglas argued that Lincoln was not a great statesman. Douglas said Lincoln, by his statement in his House Divided speech that the country could not exist half slave and half free, was encouraging war.

   STRENGTHS WEAKNESSES

[Continued on next page.]

[Continued from previous page.]

3. We want to know why the South seceded from the Union in 1861. A Trenton, New Jersey, *Gazette* article on January 3, 1861, stated that secession was the result of a conspiracy by a small number of ambitious men in the South who wanted to set up a Southern Empire under their control.

   STRENGTHS WEAKNESSES

4. Jefferson Davis, President of the Confederacy, said in a speech to the Confederate Congress on April 29, 1861, that the Northern threat to slavery was the cause of Southern secession.

   STRENGTHS WEAKNESSES

5. Historian James G. Randall said, in an article published in 1940, that there was no good reason for secession and war in 1861. He said the war was caused by poor leadership and emotional decisions.

   STRENGTHS WEAKNESSES

LESSON 20 Analyzing Cause and Effect

Connection between Cause and Effect

The Missouri Compromise of 1820 prohibited (outlawed) slavery in the territories above 36°30', which included Kansas and Nebraska. In 1854 Congress passed the controversial Kansas-Nebraska Act which voided the Missouri Compromise by allowing "popular sovereignty" in the territories. That is, the voters in the territories could vote to allow slavery where it had been prohibited by the Missouri Compromise.

This part of the lesson consists of three viewpoints, all of which argue that the Kansas-Nebraska Act led to the rise of the Republican Party.

Read the three viewpoints. As you read, note how each viewpoint makes the connection between the Kansas-Nebraska Act (the cause) and the formation of the Republican Party (the effect).

Historian A

In the 1850s Americans dreamed of building a transcontinental railroad. Senator Stephen A. Douglas wanted his home city of Chicago to be the eastern terminus (end) of the new railroad. Southerners wanted cities further south to be the terminus so those cities would prosper. To get Southern votes to support the Northern route, Senator Douglas introduced the Kansas-Nebraska Act. This Act stated that the people of Kansas and Nebraska could decide for themselves whether to allow or prohibit slavery. Kansas turned into a battleground between proslavery men and abolitionists. Some Northerners were so upset by the Act and the violence that they formed the Republican Party.

Historian B

There were four main routes proposed for the transcontinental railroad—starting from New Orleans, Memphis, St. Louis, and Chicago. Senator Stephen Douglas of Illinois wanted Chicago to be the eastern terminus. But a government survey said the southern route along the Mexican border would meet the fewest obstacles, and Senator Atchinson and his pro-Southern group in Missouri were pushing hard for St. Louis. So Senator Douglas split Nebraska into two territories and granted the people there the right to decide for themselves whether to allow or prohibit slavery. Southerners marked Kansas for slavery, and sent proslavery men into the territory. Meanwhile, abolitionists in New England organized Emigrant Aid Societies to send antislavery men to Kansas. Of course, violence soon followed. Northerners were dismayed by the violence and formed the Republican Party to oppose the extension of slavery into the territories. In the 1856 election, the Republican candidate won 114 electoral votes, which showed the growing strength of the newly formed Republican Party.

[Continued on next page.]

[Continued from previous page.]

Historian C

In early 1854 Congress passed the Kansas-Nebraska Act, which declared the Missouri Compromise void by allowing the voters in the new territories to allow or prohibit slavery there. Angry rallies were held across the North to protest the Kansas-Nebraska Act. Public meetings were also held in many states. At one such meeting at Ripon, Wisconsin, the members voted to form a new party to oppose the extension of slavery. This new party, the Republican Party, held its first meeting on July 6. It made three statements in its platform, one of which demanded the repeal of the Kansas-Nebraska Act. In the November 1854 election, the Whig Party disappeared and the Democrats, who had held a majority in Congress, now held only 83 seats in Congress to 108 for the Republicans. Of 42 Northern Democrats who voted for the Kansas-Nebraska Act, only 7 were reelected. This showed the strength of the Republican Party.

1. Which of the three viewpoints is strongest? Why do you think so? (The question is asking, "Which argument makes the strongest connection between the cause and the effect?")

Identifying Cause-and-Effect Arguments

To be cause-and-effect reasoning, a statement has to argue that something caused, led to, or brought about something else.

Label each of the following with the appropriate letter. For those items that you identify as cause-and-effect reasoning, write the cause and the effect in the space provided.

C Item illustrates **cause-and-effect** reasoning.

N Item does **not** illustrate cause-and-effect reasoning.

_______2. The local drugstore is losing business because a CVS Pharmacy opened up across the street.

CAUSE: EFFECT:

[Continued on next page.]

[Continued from previous page.]

_______3. Almost everyone who lives in a suburb more than 15 miles from a major city owns a car.

CAUSE: EFFECT:

_______4. *Uncle Tom's Cabin* aroused many Northerners to a hatred of slavery. It was a best-seller.

CAUSE: EFFECT:

_______5. In the Lincoln-Douglas debates of 1858, Senator Douglas attacked Lincoln's views on slavery in the territories.

CAUSE: EFFECT:

_______6. In 1856 John Brown led a massacre of five men at Pottawatomie Creek, a proslavery town in Kansas.

CAUSE: EFFECT:

_______7. The "Dred Scott" decision of 1857 created a storm of controversy in the United States. Antislavery people in the North were especially outraged since slavery could now spread into all the territories.

CAUSE: EFFECT:

LESSON 21 Identifying and Evaluating Types of Reasoning

Identify the type of reasoning used in each item below, then evaluate it by asking and answering the appropriate question(s). Each item may contain more than one type of reasoning. Focus your evaluation on the type of reasoning that is most central to the argument. Make diagrams to assist your evaluation when you think they would be helpful. The types of reasoning and a summary of the appropriate questions for evaluating each type of reasoning are listed below. More information can be found in the "Guide to Critical Thinking" (Unit 1).

- **Cause and Effect**—Is there a reasonable connection; might there be other possible causes; might there be important previous causes?
- **Generalization**—How large is the sample; how representative is the sample?
- **Comparison**—How are the cases similar; how are they different?

1. The railroads and canals built before the Civil War mostly ran east to west. As a result, the North and the West were drawn closer together and the South was isolated.

   Type of Reasoning:

   Evaluation:

2. Candidates in the 1840 election tried to avoid answering questions about the explosive issue of slavery, much the same as candidates today try to dodge politically sensitive issues such as abortion.

   Type of Reasoning:

   Evaluation:

[Continued on next page.]

[Continued from previous page.]

3. In the 1844 election, the Liberty Party helped the Democrat James K. Polk win by taking votes away from the Whig candidate, Henry Clay. This was especially true in New York where Polk won by a narrow margin. Had Clay won New York, he would have won the election.

   Type of Reasoning:

   Evaluation:

4. The Liberty Party got about 62,000 votes in the election of 1844, or about 2.3% of the votes cast.

   Type of Reasoning:

   Evaluation:

5. Since the South had navigable rivers for transporting goods, it had little need for railroads. In 1860 the South had only 9,000 miles of track.

   Type of Reasoning:

   Evaluation:

6. The North was hit much harder by the Panic (depression) of 1857. As a result, Northerners blamed the economic panic on an economic conspiracy by Southern congressmen to keep the tariff low. Northerners felt the tariff hurt Northern businesses.

   Type of Reasoning:

   Evaluation:

[Continued on next page.]

[Continued from previous page.]

7. In 1860 the South had a per capita income (income per person) only 73% as high as that of the North. The South was economically worse off than the North.

   Type of Reasoning:

   Evaluation:

8. John Brown's raid on Harper's Ferry, Virginia, killed all hope for compromise between North and South. To many Northerners, John Brown became a martyr, which increased their hatred for slaveholders. At the same time, the raid confirmed Southern fears that Northerners were violent and self-righteous, not interested in compromise.

   Type of Reasoning:

   Evaluation:

9. In 1860 the South had only 30% of the railroad track in the country, which shows its more backward agricultural economy.

   Type of Reasoning:

   Evaluation:

10. Most abolitionists were young adults who came from rich, elite New England families.

    Type of Reasoning:

    Evaluation:

LESSON 22 Identifying and Evaluating Proof and Debating Reasoning

This lesson focuses on two types of reasoning: proof and debating (or eliminating alternatives). Proof reasoning is further broken down into proof by evidence or example, and proof by authority.

You can identify proof by evidence by watching for evidence or factual information that is used to support an argument. You have already learned to evaluate evidence in an argument by using PROP—asking if it is a primary source, if the author of the evidence has a reason to distort, if there is other evidence to support it, and whether it is a public or private statement. Another question you need to ask of proof by evidence is, "Even if the evidence or information is true, does it actually prove the argument?"

For example, suppose Rachel is on trial for assault. If Rachel's lawyer presented strong evidence that Rachel is kind to cats, we would still feel that the evidence does not prove that she is innocent, since it has little to do with the crime.

You can recognize proof by authority by watching for appeals to a person's expertise, notoriety, or education. You can tell when a person is eliminating alternatives in an argument by watching for such cue phrases as "couldn't have been," "must have been," and "but this is wrong because." The key question for this type of reasoning is, "Have all the alternatives been eliminated?"

For example, the prosecuting attorney in a robbery case in Ohio might say, "Only Peter and Angie had a motive to commit the crime, but Peter was in Florida on the date of the crime, so Angie must have committed it." The important question is whether Peter and Angie really were the only ones with a motive to commit the crime.

When a person is arguing against an opposing point of view, that person is debating. Does the person summarize the other view fairly and are the criticisms fair?

All of these types of reasoning are explained on pp. 11–14 in the "Guide to Critical Thinking." As you identify and evaluate the items below, note especially the key questions in the boxes on pages 11 and 13. Note also the fallacies which will help you notice weaknesses in some items.

Label each of the following arguments by writing the letter on the line next to it. Then in the space below each item, evaluate it.

E The argument illustrates proof by **evidence** or example.

A The argument illustrates proof by **authority**.

D The argument illustrates **debating** or eliminating alternatives.

_______1. Candice couldn't have walked the dog. She was at the dance on Friday.

Evaluation

[Continued on next page.]

[Continued from previous page.]

_______2. The leading theatre critic in the United States gave *Phantom of the Opera* a favorable review, so it must be good.

Evaluation

_______3. One reason the North won the Civil War was due to its larger population. In almost every battle, Northern troops outnumbered Southern troops. For example, at Gettysburg, the Union forces outnumbered the Confederates by more than 20,000 men.

Evaluation

_______4. According to a respected historian, the South could have won the Civil War by fighting a guerilla war rather than sending in large armies to fight the North. Simply by holding out long enough, the South would have forced the North to give up due to the expense of trying to occupy the whole South.

Evaluation

_______5. Another historian says the historian's argument in Number 4 is wrong. This new historian says that the background of Southern leaders made the idea of guerilla warfare impossible. It never occurred to such men. Besides, the economy of the South made occupation of the region by the North a terrible burden. The South depended upon trade, so it had to stop the Union armies.

Evaluation

[Continued on next page.]

[Continued from previous page.]

_______6. The income tax began during the Civil War. According to the *Congressional Record*, the first income tax in our history was passed in August 1861.

Evaluation

_______7. There is no need to explain why the North won the Civil War. We all know the North was stronger in almost every respect.

Evaluation

_______8. Photographs taken by Mathew Brady during the war clearly show the horror of the Civil War.

Evaluation

_______9. The greatest Union general was certainly not McClellan or Meade or Halleck, it must have been Ulysses S. Grant.

Evaluation

_____10. The recent book *Vicksburg* is the best there is on the battle of Vicksburg. The historian has gathered and used more statistics on the subject than any other historian ever has.

Evaluation

LESSON 23 Which Side Caused the Firing on Fort Sumter?

Viewpoint A

Lincoln sent supply ships to reinforce Fort Sumter but told the Confederates that it was only food, and if it was not resisted, no new men, arms, or ammunition would be sent to the fort unless attacked. He was using Fort Sumter to beautifully maneuver the Confederates into firing first or backing down. The Confederates either had to attack the fort or back down and allow the North to hold the fort in their territory.

1. What is the main point of this argument?

_______2. What is the fallacy in the last sentence?

A. Correlation as cause (p. 6)

B. Prevalent proof (p. 12)

C. Composition (p. 10)

D. Either-or (p. 14)

E. Appeal to the golden mean (p. 13)

F. No fallacy

Viewpoint B

When Lincoln sent the supply ships to Fort Sumter, he was not able to control what would happen. In fact, the Confederates had more control. If Lincoln had backed down about Fort Sumter, the Southerners would have demanded Fort Pickens. After all, Fort Pickens was just as much a symbol of Northern authority in Southern territory as was Fort Sumter. The Southerners chose war, since they could have simply stopped the supply ships instead of firing on the fort.

3. What is the main point of this argument?

[Continued on next page.]

[Continued from previous page.]

_______4. What is the fallacy in the third sentence? ("If Lincoln…")

A. Correlation as cause (p. 6)

B. False scenario (p. 6)

C. Appeal to authority (p. 12)

D. Attacking the arguer (p. 14)

E. No fallacy

5. Which of these two viewpoints is stronger? Explain your answer.

LESSON 24 What Do Historians Assume about the Causes of War?

Part 1— Causes of War

Answer the following questions.

1. Are wars ever justified? Explain your answer.

2. Are wars caused by specific events or underlying reasons? Explain.

3. Rank the following as to their importance in causing wars in general. Put a 1 next to the most important cause of wars, 2 next to the second most important cause, and so on.

________ Slogans—People stop thinking about complex issues and start believing in simple slogans, such as "Remember the Maine!"

________ Moral issues—People see a great evil taking place and are willing to fight to stop it.

________ Politics—The normal compromise of politics breaks down, and political leaders are left with no real alternative to fighting to resolve a crisis.

________ Poor leadership—Leaders come along who play on the emotions, especially fear, of the public in order to gain personal power. These demagogues tend to exaggerate the evil nature of the opposing side, which leads to war. Or, leaders' poor decisions lead to needless wars.

________ Economics—People fight mainly when their economic well-being or an important resource is threatened. Or, they fight in order to take economic control over another country or region.

________ Power—People or leaders fight to enhance their country's, and their own, power.

________ Other—

[Continued on next page.]

[Continued from previous page.]

4. Discuss your rankings with your classmates. Is everyone's ranking the same? How would your beliefs about the causes of war in general influence the way you research the causes of the Civil War? That is, if you believed that most wars were caused mainly by moral issues and a classmate believed most wars were caused mainly by poor leadership, how would your research by different from your classmate's research?

5. Your rankings are really presuppositions or general assumptions about war. How do you think you arrived at your assumptions about war? Think of articles or books you've read, things you've discussed in history or other classes, newscasts you've watched about recent wars, movies you've seen involving war, and friends or relatives who may have influenced you.

6. What factors and/or experiences in historians' backgrounds might influence their views of the causes of war? List three.

Part II— Thucydides and the Causes of the Peloponnesian War

Thucydides (pronounced *thyoo SID ih deez*) was a historian who wrote about a great war in Ancient Greece. Read the excerpt below from *History of the Peloponnesian War, Book I*, page 25, and answer the questions which follow.

> War began when the Athenians and the Peloponnesians broke the Thirty Years Truce which had been made after the capture of Euboea. As to the reasons why they broke the truce, I propose first to give an account of the causes of complaint which they had against each other and of specific instances (times) where their interests clashed; this is in order that there should be no doubt in anyone's mind about what led to this great war falling upon the Hellenes (Greeks). But the real reason for the war is, in my opinion, most likely to be disguised by such an
>
> *[Continued on next page.]*

[Continued from previous page.]
argument. What made war inevitable was the growth of Athenian power and the fear which this caused in Sparta. As for the reasons for breaking the truce and declaring war which were openly expressed by each side, they are as follows... [He goes on to explain the reasons for breaking the truce.]

7. Check off the statements with which Thucydides would probably have agreed:

_______a. Events have a number of causes.

_______b. Men do not control events. Fate or the gods punish and reward people.

_______c. Causes can be ranked by order of importance.

______d. War is inevitable.

_______e. This war had political and economic causes.

8. To what extent do you agree with Thucydides' view of history? Explain your answer.

Part III— Interpretations of the Civil War

Below are short summaries of major interpretations of the causes of the Civil War. Read them and then answer the questions that follow.

Interpretation A (1861–1900)

The peace of the Union was broken by the fanatical abolitionists who conspired to destroy the Southern way of life. The publication of *The Liberator* by William Lloyd Garrison, as well as the formation of antislavery societies, kept agitation against the South strong. *Uncle Tom's Cabin* increased the agitation. The South, which loved the Union, merely wished to be let alone with proper respect, under the Constitution, for its local institutions. After all, the Constitution was a compact (agreement) among the states. Southerners exerted states' rights and withdrew from the compact that was already broken by Northern violation of their rights as states under the Constitution. Northern agitation forced the South to secede, and later to fight, in self-defense.

[Continued on next page.]

[Continued from previous page.]

Interpretation B (1861–1900)

The Civil War was brought on by a conspiracy of slaveholders to rule the Union or break it. The conspirators were determined to force the nation to accept slavery not only in the South, but in the territories and eventually in the Northern states as well. The conspiracy began with exclusion of free discussion of slavery in the South. Then Congress passed the gag resolution, which prevented antislavery petitions from being received in Congress. The obnoxious Fugitive Slave Act was forced upon the unwilling North. Proslavery senators next helped get the Kansas-Nebraska Act passed, which repealed the Missouri Compromise. Then slaveholders organized to capture Kansas for slavery. The Dred Scott Case, which allowed a slave to be taken anywhere in the territories, had reached the Supreme Court. Finally, the slavocracy conspired in 1860 to split the Democratic Party so Lincoln would get elected. This allowed them to force secession on Southern Unionists. The rebel conspiracy had succeeded in bringing on the Civil War.

Interpretation C (1865–1900)

The Civil War was an irrepressible (inevitable) conflict between slavery and freedom. The abolitionists were a natural response to the evils of slavery. The North had a moral obligation to wipe out slavery. The abolitionists agitated to end slavery and slaveholders tried to stop them. All the major events before 1861 involved slavery—Compromise of 1850, Kansas-Nebraska Act, *Uncle Tom's Cabin*, Dred Scott Case, John Brown's Raid, Lincoln's election, and, of course, secession.

Interpretation D (1892)

Stephen A. Douglas broke the peace by sponsoring the foolish Kansas-Nebraska Act of 1854. The Act gave the South hope that they could get the slave states above the 36°30' line of the Missouri Compromise. Meanwhile, it infuriated Northerners by voiding a compromise which had helped preserve peace for thirty-four years. The Act unleashed the forces of war by bringing, for the first time, slaveholders and abolitionists into the same state. Naturally violence resulted in what came to be known as "bleeding Kansas." The era of compromises was at an end, and the period of violence began, which escalated to war.

Interpretation E (1917–1930)

The Civil War was brought on by a difference in cultures between the more industrialized, urbanized, small farm North, and the plantation culture of the South. Southerners romanticized farming as a way of life and, therefore, saw change as a threat. Leisure time, family, and honor were important values. Making money was not. Materialism and urbanization were bad; competition emphasized selfishness. The North, meanwhile, emphasized competition, progress, making money, economic growth, and the work ethic, all of which implied change. With such diametrically opposed sets of life-styles and values, the war was inevitable.

[Continued on next page.]

[Continued from previous page.]

Interpretation F (1917–1930)

The decline of national parties and the rise of sectional parties in the 1850s meant that the political system designed for compromise had broken down. Normally, each political party represents broad, diverse interests which forces it to take moderate positions on controversial issues. Sectional parties in the 1850s had the opposite effect; each party took extreme positions and represented only a sectional interest. When Lincoln was elected in 1860, the South realized it had lost the struggle for control and seceded. War followed soon thereafter.

Interpretation G (1927–1940)

The Civil War was a result of the economic conflict between the industrial North and the agrarian South. The North wanted government support for transportation and banking, along with a high protective tariff. The South was opposed to these policies. In the 1850s the South had control of the government, but in the 1860 election, the North gained control of the presidency. The North thereby overthrew the agrarian, aristocratic South in what should be called the second American Revolution.

Interpretation H (1921–1937)

Abraham Lincoln's actions and policies brought on the Civil War. Lincoln was a shrewd politician who wanted to be president and who wanted to keep his party strong. His "house divided" speech put him on record against a nation half slave and half free, which implied the need for war, if necessary. In the Lincoln-Douglas debates, Lincoln took a position rigidly against expansion of slavery in the territories when, as Douglas repeatedly pointed out, slavery couldn't expand into those territories. Lincoln was inflaming something that wasn't a real issue. After he was elected, Lincoln refused compromise efforts to preserve peace and, against the advice of his advisers, he resupplied Fort Sumter, which led directly to the war.

Interpretation I (1919–1940)

The Civil War was unnecessary. A generation of poor leaders and fanatics on both sides blundered into a war that should never have been fought. Slavery was dying anyway, and there was no other cause sufficient for fighting.

Interpretation J (1945–1950)

Slavery was a moral evil requiring moral people to oppose it. The rise of abolitionists was a natural response to slavery. When the South resisted the call for abolition of slavery and then seceded, the North was justified in fighting to destroy the institution.

[Continued on next page.]

[Continued from previous page.]

Interpretation K (1960s)

Religion was a key factor in bringing on the Civil War. Devoutly religious people became abolitionists. Further, statistical investigation of voting shows that a high percentage of those who voted for Abraham Lincoln were members of churches. These deeply religious people wanted religious revival including ridding the country of slavery.

Interpretation L (1980s)

The Civil War was caused partly by our political institutions. If we had only one house in our legislature with representation based on free population only, or if the constitution could have been amended more easily, the South would have been forced to secede much earlier, perhaps in the 1820s. Since issues would not have festered for so long, and the bloodshed of the 1850s would not have occurred, war would probably have been avoided.

Questions about the Interpretations

9. Pick any two interpretations and make a hypothesis about the general assumptions those historians make about the causes of war. (Remember to phrase assumptions in general terms, i.e., "When people don't...they get into wars.") See the list of possible assumptions about war in question 3 (p. 160) for ideas on assumptions.

INTERPRETATION	ASSUMPTIONS ABOUT THE CAUSES OF WAR

10. What do you notice about the early interpretations of the war (A, B, C)? What do they seem to emphasize?

11. How did events at the time of writing influence either Interpretation I or J?

[Continued on next page.]

[Continued from previous page.]

12. Why do different historians emphasize different events in their interpretations of the causes of the Civil War?

13. Which of the interpretations is weakest? Explain your answer.

14. In general, how have interpretations of the causes of the Civil War changed over the past 120 years?

Part IV

Read the following explanation of the cause the Civil War and then explain what's wrong with this explanation.

> In the Compromise of 1850, the North got an extra free state, which angered the Southerners, while the South got a Fugitive Slave Law, which angered the North. In 1852 *Uncle Tom's Cabin* was published. It sold 300,000 copies in the first year and influenced many Northerners to oppose slavery. The Kansas-Nebraska Act of 1854 made many Northerners upset since it repealed the Missouri Compromise. In the 1850s the political parties became sectional—the Republicans were strong in the North and the Democrats were strong in the South. The South wanted and got a lower tariff. Soon thereafter, in 1857, an economic recession hit the North. Many Northerners blamed their bad economic times on the lower tariff. When Lincoln was elected in 1860, Southern leaders felt they had no choice but to secede from the Union. War broke out in 1861 at Fort Sumter.

15. What's wrong with this explanation of the causes of the Civil War?

LESSON 25 What Were the Causes of the Civil War?

As was shown in Lesson 24, historians do not agree on the main cause of the Civil War. This lesson presents summaries of the views of four historians. Read them and answer the questions that follow.

Historian A (1913)

(1) There is a risk in arguing that any historic event was due to a single cause. Nevertheless, for the Civil War, it may safely be argued that there was a single cause, slavery. If the Negro had never been brought to America, our Civil War could not have occurred.

(2) Differences over the tariff were not an important cause of the war. In 1832 South Carolina nullified the tariff acts passed in 1828 and 1832. No other state joined in the nullification, and the issue was settled peacefully. The American Union could not be broken by a tariff dispute.

(3) At the time of the Constitution in 1789, the North and South were not very different. A number of Southerners felt slavery was wrong and should be abolished gradually. Then the cotton gin was invented which made slavery profitable. Southern opinion changed. Slavery was seen as a great religious and moral blessing.

(4) In 1831 William Lloyd Garrison began his crusade against slavery. In *The Liberator*, he preached that slavery was wrong. Though his active followers were never many, he got people thinking that slavery was wrong. In the nineteen years before 1850, antislavery sentiment in the North constantly increased.

(5) Part of the Compromise of 1850 was the Fugitive Slave Act. The law presumed that a black was a runaway slave until he could prove otherwise, which ran counter to the American legal belief in innocence until proven guilty. Further, the commissioner who would decide the matter received $10 if he decided the Negro was a runaway slave and only $5 if he held the Negro to be a freeman. Many Northerners were outraged by these provisions of the Fugitive Slave Act.

(6) The controversy over the morality of slavery rose to a new level with the 1852 publication of *Uncle Tom's Cabin*. The novel sold a million and a half copies in England and the United States, and it was performed as a play in London and Paris. The election of Lincoln in 1860 was a great factor in the destruction of slavery, and, in gaining votes for Lincoln, *Uncle Tom's Cabin* was an important cause of the war.

(7) The North was further inflamed by the Kansas-Nebraska Act of 1854, which voided the Missouri Compromise and allowed for the expansion of slavery into the territories. Senator Chase, an opponent of the bill, said, "They [Southerners] celebrate a present victory but the echoes they awake will never rest until slavery itself shall die." The Kansas-Nebraska Act roused antislavery feeling in the country, and led to the formation of the Republican Party: a party to unite Whigs, antislavery

[Continued on next page.]

Historian A

[Continued from previous page.]

Democrats, and Free-Soilers in their resistance to slave power.

(8) Then in the Dred Scott Case, the Supreme Court decided that slaves could be taken anywhere in the territories. Parties and leaders split over the slavery issue. In 1858 Senator William H. Seward declared that there existed "an irrepressible [inevitable] conflict" between slavery and freedom.

(9) Towards the end of 1859, John Brown led his violent attack on slavery by capturing the United States arsenal at Harper's Ferry, Virginia. The attempt, of course, failed. Brown and four of his followers were taken prisoner. He had a fair trial and was hanged forty-five days later. Southerners believed that Brown had "whetted knives of butchery for their mothers, sisters, daughters, and babes." To many Northerners he became a martyr. Northern soldiers were inspired by the stirring music and words:

"John Brown's body lies a-moldering in the grave, but his soul goes marching on."

(10) The final break came in the election of 1860. Republican Abraham Lincoln won by carrying all the free states except New Jersey, while he did not receive a single vote in ten out of the eleven states that later seceded and made up the Southern Confederacy. The day after the election, the legislature of South Carolina called a convention. Leaders argued in speeches that the North had made an attack on slavery, their sacred institution. They concluded that the only way they could preserve their liberty and property was by separation from the Union. The Civil War began soon after.

Historian B (1927)

(1) The economic systems of the North and South were very different in the decades before the Civil War. Had the economic systems of the two regions remained unchanged or changed slowly, the balance of power might have been maintained indefinitely and the Civil War avoided. But the American economy did not remain static. The economic changes increased the tension between North and South, which brought on the war.

(2) As the industrial North expanded in production and area, businessmen demanded a high tariff to protect against foreign competition as well as government financial help (especially in building transportation) for manufacturing and trade expansion. Southerners, meanwhile, with their plantation economy, were opposed to the higher prices the tariff would bring and did not want to pay higher taxes to help manufacturers in the North.

(3) Under these circumstances, the South viewed the Whigs and later the Republicans as parties set up to enrich the North at the financial expense of the South. Reuben Davis of Mississippi complained in 1860, "There is not a pursuit [business] in which man is engaged (agriculture excepted) which is not demanding legislative aid to enable it to enlarge its profits, and all at the expense of

[Continued on next page.]

Historian B

[Continued from previous page.]

the primary pursuit of men—agriculture. Those interests, having a common purpose of plunder, have united and combined to use the government as the instrument of their operation....Now this combined host of interests stands arrayed against the agricultural states...."

(4) The agitation in the North against slavery provided Southerners with further proof of a Northern conspiracy against the agricultural South. Northerners in the Free-Soil Party didn't want to free slaves everywhere, just prevent slavery from spreading to the territories.

(5) Senator Jefferson Davis charged Northern Senators with using slavery as an excuse: "What do you propose, gentlemen of the Free-Soil Party?...You say you are opposed to the expansion of slavery....Is the slave benefited by it? Not at all. It is not humanity that influences you....It is that you may have an opportunity of cheating us that you want to limit slave territory within circumscribed bounds. It is that you may have a majority in the Congress of the United States and convert the Government into an engine of northern aggrandizement [enrichment]....You desire to weaken the political power of the Southern states; and why? Because you want, by an unjust system of legislation, to promote the industry of the New England states, at the expense of the people of the South and their industry."

(6) Republicans, like Free-Soilers also opposed only the expansion of slavery. Abraham Lincoln said emphatically that the Republicans didn't intend to interfere with slavery in the states. The only political party to propose abolition of slavery was the Liberty Party, which received only 2.5% of the vote in the 1844 election. This shows that the moral issue of slavery was not an important cause of the Civil War.

(7) The slave owners fought to get control of the government against the growing population of the North. In Northern eyes, the slave owners were able to check Northern power by gaining control of the Democratic Party and the government in the 1850s, the decade before the Civil War. William H. Seward of New York claimed the slaveholders controlled the key committees in the Senate, and he saw no great champion of freedom in the House. He accused the President of being "a confessed apologist of the slave-property class," and noted that the Supreme Court consisted of a majority of justices from the South.

(8) Democratic control of the government after 1852 was confirmed in a series of events which indicated an indefinite expansion of slavery into the territories and a withdrawal of government support from industrial and commercial enterprise. First Congress repealed the Missouri Compromise, throwing open the Louisiana Purchase to slavery. Then in the "Ostend Manifesto," proslavery leaders declared the United States would be justified to take Cuba (a plantation economy) from Spain by force. In the Dred Scott Case of 1857, Southern Chief Justice Taney declared that Congress had no power to prohibit slavery in the territories at any time.

[Continued on next page.]

Historian B

[Continued from previous page.]

(9) On economic matters, in 1859 Congress stopped the last of government subsidies for steamship companies. In 1857 the tariff was reduced. Immediately an industrial panic (a depression) burst upon the country. Many Northerners blamed the economic distress on the low tariff pushed through by Southern Democrats.

(10) But Southern control of the national government could not last. Steadily the capitalist North increased in numbers and strength compared to the South. Finally, in 1860, the Republican Abraham Lincoln was elected President. Northern businessmen and industrialists would get what they wanted: federal grants to build a transcontinental railroad, high tariffs, government help for banking and other businesses. To Southern leaders the choice was clear—stay in the Union and be plundered by the North, or secede (withdraw) from the Union.

(11) With secession came the irrepressible conflict in 1861—the Civil War. By it the capitalists, laborers, and farmers of the North and West drove the Southern plantation owners from power in the national government. The Civil War was really the second American Revolution, an economic revolution by which the capitalists gained dominance over the slave owners and pushed industrialization forward.

Historian C (1929, 1940)

(1) Some people have idealized the Civil War. One writer called it "the last romantic war." But historians must deal with reality. The numbers of killed and wounded in the Civil War are staggering. The surgeon general reported 315,555 soldier graves of which 145,000 were unidentified graves.[1] To the soldiers who contracted pneumonia, malaria, typhus, and other diseases, the war could hardly have looked romantic. In fact, the very word "war" does not really capture the realism of it. A better term would be "organized murder" or "human slaughterhouse."

(2) The generation of the 1850s blundered into the ghastly, indecisive slaughter. There was no sufficient cause for the Civil War—not slavery, not economics, not cultural differences, nothing. It was a repressible conflict—a needless war.

(3) Slavery certainly did not cause the war. Slavery had reached the limit of its geographic growth by 1860. The northern line of Arkansas was the northern limit of slavery, and the Mississippi River, except for Texas, was the western limit. Anyone who examines the matter objectively realizes that slavery would never really spread to Kansas or Nebraska.[2] The census of 1860 showed two slaves in Kansas and fifteen in Nebraska. Likewise, in the Mexican Cession (New Mexico, Utah, Nevada, Colorado, Arizona, and California) slavery was blocked by soil, climate, and cheap native labor. California became a free

[Continued on next page.]

Historian C

[Continued from previous page.]

state, and the 1860 Census did not list a single slave in New Mexico, Colorado, or Nevada.

(4) The issue about slave and free states was dead by 1860, but people couldn't see it. There was still opportunity for politicians to play on people's prejudice and fear. In terms of slave states in the West, the North fought for what it could get without fighting, and the South fought for what it could never get.

(5) Even in the South itself, slavery was dying by 1860. There was a great increase in cotton production, especially after 1858, which forced the price of cotton down. Prices of slaves would have had to drop then; since slaves would have been less valuable as cotton became less profitable. Cotton lands did actually become unprofitable after the Civil War, which shows that slave prices really would have dropped after 1861. Southerners would have economic incentive to get rid of their now costly labor force. They may have switched to a seasonal, free labor force. In any event, they surely would not have fought to the death to save slavery.

(6) The other traditional explanations for the Civil War also fail the test of careful examination. Economic diversity between the industrializing North and plantation South offered as much motive for union as for secession. Northern textile mills needed Southern cotton and Southern plantations needed Northern manufactured goods. The sectional tariff was an issue, but it's always a sectional issue, and there haven't been wars over it at other times, so why would it have caused war only in 1861?

(7) No explanation is sufficient for the Civil War without considering bogus leadership, poor judgment, emotional unreason, misunderstanding, misrepresentation of the other side, fanaticism. Several examples illustrate how illogical people were in blundering into war. Southerner Robert Toombs said he would resist Stephen A. Douglas though he could see "nothing but...defeat in the future."[3] He was choosing war though he knew the South would lose. Henry Watterson, an antislavery unionist, fought for the Confederacy because he was from Tennessee, which was certainly an emotional rather than a rational decision. Some people had an unrealistic view of war. Ralph Waldo Emerson said, "War is a realist, shatters everything flimsy and shifty, sets aside all false issues...breaks through all that is not real."[4]

(8) With such unrealistic, emotional views, the country blundered into a needless war in 1861. Historians then went back searching for causes, assuming there were sufficient causes for war. If the dispute with England over Oregon in the 1840s had ended in war, historians would have gone back searching for differences leading to war, neglecting friendly factors. When crises pass without wars, people go back to normal, recognizing how artificial and unimportant the issues had been that were inflamed by the small minority of agitators and unscrupulous politicians. Such was the case with the Civil War.

[Continued on next page.]

[Continued from previous page.]

Endnotes for Historian C

1. Joseph K. Barnes, ed. *The Medical and Surgical History of the War of the Rebellion* (Washington, second issue, 1875), Pt. 1, Vol. I, Intro p. xxxiii.
2. It is clear that Senator Stephen A. Douglas believed that neither Nebraska nor Kansas would ever become a slave state. See quotations from his speeches in Albert J. Beveridge, *Abraham Lincoln, 1809–1858* (Boston, 1928), pp. 108, 193.
3. Ulrich B. Phillips, ed. "The Correspondence of Robert Toombs, Alexander H. Stephens, and Howell Cobbs" in *American Historical Association, Annual Report*, 1911 (Washington, 1913), II. p. 469.
4. Edward W. Emerson and Waldo E. Forbes, eds., *Journals of Ralph Waldo Emerson* (Boston, 1909), IX, p. 461.

Historian D (1949)

(1) Revisionist historians (one of them Historian C) have suggested that the Civil War was not inevitable, but rather that it was the result of a blundering generation which let emotions interfere with peacefully solving the problems of the 1850s. These historians assert that slavery was not the cause of war. They argue that the slavery problem could have been solved without war. It would be fruitful, therefore, to examine whether slavery could have been abolished without war.

(2) Reform of slavery by Southerners was not possible. Southern slaveholders united in defense of slavery in response to abolitionist challenges and would not even consider ending it in any way. Revisionists cannot say that there should not have been abolitionists, because abolitionism was an inevitable result of slavery. It is like saying there should have been no anti-Nazis in the 1930s. Besides, no part of the South made substantial progress toward ending slavery even before abolitionism began. It is extremely unlikely that Southerners would ever have voluntarily done away with slavery.

(3) Revisionists say that the Southern economy based on slavery was declining in the 1850s and would have died without the Civil War. This view is based on the assumption that slaveholders would have recognized the cause of their problem and moved to abolish slavery in response. However, this is not what Southerners had done up to the Civil War. They had always blamed hard times on Northern exploitations, not on their system. Southerners were not ready to give up their slave system.

(4) So the slave system was not to be given up lightly by the slaveholders. And the slave system was evil. Moreover, in acting to eliminate criticism of its peculiar institution (slavery), the South outlawed what a believer in democracy can only regard as the basic values of man—free speech and dissent.

(5) A society bent on defending its evil institutions thus creates moral differences far too profound to be solved by compromise. Such a society forces upon everyone, both those living at the time and those historians writing about it later, the necessity for a moral judgment or action.

(6) Because the revisionist historians felt no moral urgency to end slavery, they called the abolitionists "fanatics." But the "fanatics" had good moral

[Continued on next page.]

Historian D

[Continued from previous page.]

reasons for opposing slavery. It was the moral issue of slavery, for example, that gave significance to the debate over slavery in the territories and over the enforcement of the fugitive slave laws. The evidence shows that these issues, by themselves, were not the basic issues. But they were the available issues; and they became charged with the moral significance of the central issue of slavery.

(7) In light of the expansion of Nazi-ism and its wanton attacks on innocent countries in the past decade, are we to conclude, as the revisionists do, that man can solve peaceably all the problems which overwhelm him? Will we be condemned someday by historians as another blundering generation? Should we have tried at all costs to settle our disagreements with Hitler peacefully?

(8) We delude ourselves when we think that history teaches us that evil will be "outmoded" by progress and that politics consequently does not impose on us the necessity for moral decision and for struggle.

Worksheet for Lesson 25

Historian A

1. What is the main point of Historian A's interpretation?

2. How strong is Historian A's cause-and-effect reasoning?

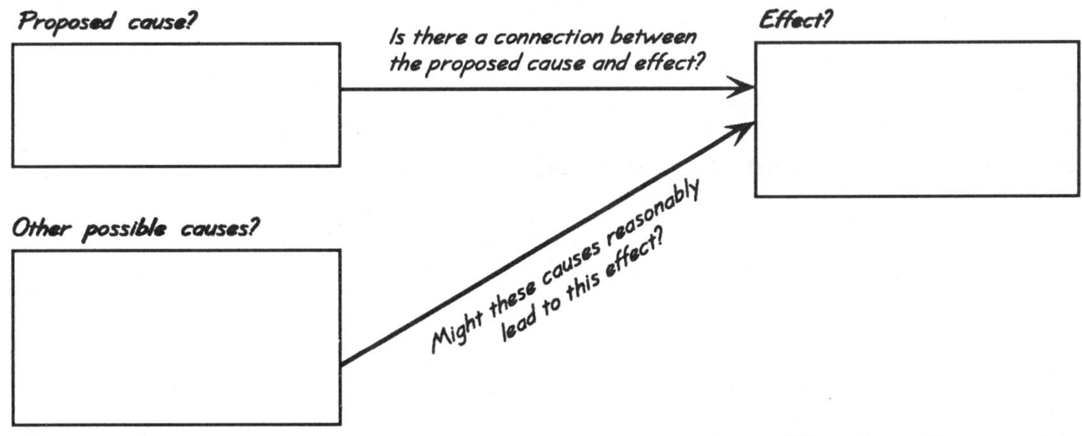

[Continued on next page.]

[Continued from previous page.]

3. Evaluate one generalization that Historian A makes.

4. Evaluate one piece of evidence Historian A uses.

5. Overall, how strong is the evidence in this argument?

6. How strong is Historian A's interpretation? Why do you think so?

Q Historian B

7. What is the main point of Historian B's interpretation?

8. How strong is Historian B's cause-and-effect reasoning?

[Continued on next page.]

[Continued from previous page.]

9. Evaluate the reasoning in the last sentence of Paragraph 9.

10. Evaluate one piece of evidence used by Historian B.

11. How strong is Historian B's interpretation? Why do you think so?

Q Historian C

12. What is the main point of Historian C's interpretation?

13. Evaluate Historian C's cause-and-effect reasoning.

14. Evaluate the argument in Paragraph 3.

15. Evaluate one piece of Historian C's evidence.

[Continued on next page.]

[Continued from previous page.]

16. How strong is Historian C's interpretation? Why do you think so?

Historian D

17. What is the main point of Historian D's interpretation?

18. Evaluate the reasoning used in the third and fourth sentences of Paragraph 2. (Starts with, "Revisionists cannot...")

19. Evaluate the cause-and-effect reasoning in this interpretation.

20. How strong is Historian D's interpretation? Why do you think so?

General Question

21. How do you think the date of publication of each interpretation affected the historian's viewpoint? Explain your answer.

LESSON 26 What Led to the Emancipation Proclamation and England's Neutrality in the Civil War?

Part A—Why Did President Lincoln Issue the Emancipation Proclamation?

In December 1862, President Lincoln issued the Emancipation Proclamation, which basically said that slaves were freed in those states which were still in rebellion against the Union (that is, the Confederate States).

Theory A

Lincoln issued the Emancipation Proclamation to keep abolitionists on the Northern side and to raise Northern morale.

Theory B

Lincoln issued the Emancipation Proclamation to raise Northern Morale, use Northern industry to its fullest advantage, and keep the border states on the Northern side.

Theory C

Lincoln issued the Emancipation Proclamation to get England and France to remain neutral and to capitalize on (make use of) the Northern victory at Antietam.

Theory D

Lincoln issued the Emancipation Proclamation to get England and France to remain neutral and to raise Northern morale.

Theory E

Lincoln issued the Emancipation Proclamation to get England and France to remain neutral, to neutralize the advantage of Southern military leaders, and to embarrass England, since England had been involved with slavery.

[Continued on next page.]

[Continued from previous page.]

Part B—Why Didn't England Side with the South?

During the Civil War the South tried to get England to openly side with it against the North. England gave some support to the South and considered siding with the Confederacy but never actually did side with it.

Theory A

No country wants to join sides with a loser, and after the Battle of Antietam, England hesitated to side with the South. Then, after the Emancipation Proclamation, England found it very difficult to join the South since so many English citizens would have opposed fighting to defend slavery.

Theory B

England's monarchy was leaning toward the South, but when it appeared that the South might not win, the monarchy decided to stay out of the war. After all, the North was stronger industrially.

Theory C

England needed Northern wheat more than it needed Southern cotton. In addition, since Northern morale was lower than Southern morale and since unemployment in England wasn't very high, she decided not to help the South in the war.

Theory D

England did not need Southern cotton that badly. When the Southerners won the Battle of Bull Run, England didn't think that the South needed much help. Then, when Lincoln issued the Emancipation Proclamation, England couldn't side with the South since so many of her citizens would have been opposed to fighting to defend slavery.

[Continued on next page.]

[Continued from previous page.]

Relevant Information

Assume that the information that follows is true.

A. England needed Southern cotton to keep its textile mills going. When cotton was cut off by the American (Northern) blockade, unemployment went up.

B. Border states (Maryland, Kentucky, and Missouri) sided with the North early in the war, partly because the North had said it was fighting to preserve the Union, not abolish slavery. Many people in the border states owned slaves.

C. Even monarchies have difficulty fighting unpopular wars.

D. The morale of Southern soldiers was high because they believed they were protecting their homeland from invasion.

E. The North was more industrialized than the South.

F. The Battle of Antietam was fought in September 1862, and, strategically, it was a great Northern victory.

G. Very few people in the North were abolitionists, and there were even fewer abolitionists in the border states.

H. The South only had to fight to a draw in order to win the war. If the North could not defeat her, then the South would be independent.

I. England built ships for the South to run the Northern blockade.

J. Northern soldiers by 1862 had lost enthusiasm for fighting to save the Union. Some soldiers felt the Union wasn't worth dying for.

K. Monarchies are usually opposed to rebellions, such as the Southern rebellion in the Civil War.

L. Northern Democrats felt slavery should not be the issue over which the war was to be fought.

M. The South, on a whole, had better military leaders than did the North.

N. Most people throughout the world, including the Northern United States, England, and France, opposed slavery.

O. England needed Northern wheat during the 1860s, since she had a food shortage.

P. There had been slavery in England, but by 1860, England had abolished it.

Q. The South won the Battle of Chancellorsville in the spring of 1863.

R. The aristocrats in England and France were sympathetic to the South (since the South was more aristocratic and the North was more democratic) and were important in persuading the governments to seriously consider siding with the South in 1862.

[Continued on next page.]

Relevant Information

[Continued from previous page.]

S. Abolitionists were very devoted to their cause (ending slavery).

T. France was quite interested in increasing its influence in Mexico in the 1860s.

U. The South won a decisive victory at Bull Run in August 1862.

V. Workers in England disliked the South because they hated the idea of slavery.

W. England was a monarchy.

Worksheet

Part A

1. Write down the strengths and weaknesses of each theory on why President Lincoln issued the Emancipation Proclamation. Write the letter(s) of the relevant information that weaken or strengthen each theory and explain why.

Theory	Weaknesses	Strengths
	Write the letter of any Relevant Information that weakens the theory and explain why.	Write the letter of any Relevant Information that strengthens the theory and explain why.
Theory A		
Theory B		
Theory C		
Theory D		
Theory E		

[Continued on next page.]

[Continued from previous page.]

2. Which theory on why President Lincoln issued the Emancipation Proclamation is strongest? Why do you think so?

3. Suppose you learned that in the summer of 1862, Lincoln was hoping to issue a dramatic statement on slavery. However, he was concerned that with the war going so badly for the North, any statement would look like an act of desperation by the losing side, and only further weaken the Northern cause. Which theory does this information support most directly? Why do you think so?

4. Marxist historians believe that economics and the struggle between social classes are the most important aspects of history. For example, they feel that the aristocrats (nobles) had most of the power during feudalism. The aristocrats were overthrown by the capitalists (bourgeoisie), which started capitalism. They, in turn, will be overthrown by the workers (proletariats), which will mark the state of socialism. Which two pieces of relevant information would be most important to a Marxist historian? Explain your answer.

5. Based on what you have learned about the Emancipation Proclamation, write a generalization about some of the things political leaders consider in making important decisions. Start your statement with, “Political leaders tend to....”

[Continued on next page.]

[Continued from previous page.]

Part B

6. Write down the strengths and weaknesses of each theory on why England did not side with the South in the Civil War. Write the letter(s) of the relevant information that weaken or strengthen each theory and explain why.

Theory	Weaknesses	Strengths
	Write the letter of any Relevant Information that weakens the theory and explain why.	Write the letter of any Relevant Information that strengthens the theory and explain why.
Theory A		
Theory B		
Theory C		
Theory D		

7. Which theory is strongest? Why do you think so?

8. Based upon what you have learned about why England decided not to side with the South during the Civil War, how accurate do you think the following generalization is?

   "Political leaders are very aware of public opinion when they make important decisions."

LESSON 27 What Role Did Racism Play in the Civil War and Nineteenth-Century America?

Part I

Below are some stereotypes of blacks in the nineteenth century. Write what you think the purpose of each stereotype was. What were those who made up or used the stereotype hoping to accomplish or to communicate? The time period given is an important clue to the stereotype.

	STEREOTYPE	PURPOSE
1 Sambo	In the early 1800s, the Sambo stereotype took hold. Sambo was a happy, obedient, childlike, rather lazy slave. The stereotype persisted up to the 1930s in movies in which blacks continued to be portrayed as lazy and irresponsible.	
2 Uncle Ned	The song "Uncle Ned" was popular among Southern whites in the 1870s: "There was an old darkie and they called him Uncle Ned. And he died long ago, long ago. And he had no wool on the top of his head. In the place where the wool ought to grow. So lay down the shovel and the hoe. And hang up the fiddle and the bow. No more hard work for poor old Uncle Ned. He's gone where the good darkies go."	
3 Zip Coon	This stereotype began before the Civil War and was popular in the 1860s and 1870s. Zip Coon was a free black who dressed in fine clothes and used big words. But he was overdressed, often with clothes that didn't match. And he misused the big words. This theatre character was a buffoon whom audiences found quite humorous.	
4 The Savage	After the Civil War, a new stereotype began showing blacks as savages. Blacks were shown with spears around fires. The stereotype peaked in the 1915 film "Birth of a Nation" in which black men chased white virgins. In one scene a white virgin jumped to her death rather than submit to one of these black savages.	
5 Mammy	The mammy stereotype began during slavery and persisted in movies up to the 1950s and in Aunt Jemima pancakes and syrup. Mammy was a very fat, happy, loyal slave devoted to her last drop of blood to her owner's family. She was a hard worker who wore a bandanna covering her hair. She was strong-willed and often had a big influence on the master's family.	
6 Picaninny	In the late 1800s, the stereotype of unclothed black children, or picaninnies, was popular as book illustrations and on postcards. Later the stereotype was used in movies. Picaninnies were shown in nature—in trees near water—and most often being pursued by alligators. In one movie a picaninny was eaten by an alligator. A poem about picaninnies entitled "Five Little Niggers" showed them dying or disappearing one by one.	

[Continued on next page.]

[Continued from previous page.]

Part II—Race Relations during the Civil War

 Below is some information on relations between whites and blacks during the Civil War. Read it and answer the questions that follow.

Source A

Letter by A. Davenport (a Union soldier from New York) to his family, June 19, 1861

"I think that the best way to settle the question of what to do with the darkies would be to shoot them."

Source B

New York Tribune, August 16, 1862 (Letter to the Editor)

"I am quite sure there is not one man in ten but would feel himself degraded as a volunteer if negro equality is to be the order in the field of battle...."

Source C

Letter by Abraham Lincoln to the Religious Denominations of Chicago, September 13, 1862

"If we were to arm them [blacks], I fear that in a few weeks the arms would be in the hands of the rebels; and, indeed, thus far we have not had arms enough to equip our white troops...."

Source D

Reminiscence of a former black soldier in the Union Army

"At first the faintest intimation that Negroes should be employed as soldiers in the Union Army was met with derision. By many it was regarded as a joke. The idea of arming the ex-slaves seemed ridiculous to most civil and military officers....

"Most observing and thoughtful people concluded that centuries of servitude had rendered the Negro slave incapable of any civil or military service....Some officers talked of resigning if Negroes were to be called upon to fight battles of a free republic."

[Continued on next page.]

[Continued from previous page.]

Source E

Fragment of a letter from Peter Welsh, a Union soldier in the 28th Regiment, Massachusetts Volunteers, early 1863

"The feeling against nigars is intensely strong in this army [Union] as is plainly to be seen wherever and whenever they meet them. They are looked upon as the principal cause of this war, and this feeling is especially strong in the Irish regiments."

Source F

Letter from Tighlman Jones (a Union soldier) to Brother Zillman Jones, October 6, 1863

"You have heard of Negroes being enlisted to fight for Uncle Sam. If you would like to know what the [white] soldiers think about the idea, I can almost tell you. Why, that is just what they desire. There is some soldiers who curse and blow and make great noise about it, but we set him as a convalescent who is like a man who is afraid of smallpox....I think more of a Negro Union soldier than I do of all the cowardly Copperhead trash of the North [Copperheads were Northerners who opposed the war]...."

Source G

Editorial, *New York Times*, March 7, 1864

"There has been no more striking manifestation of the marvelous times that are upon us than the scene in our streets at the departure of the first of our colored regiments.

"Eight months ago the African race in this city were literally hunted down like wild beasts [in the New York Draft Riot of 1863, the rioters were mostly working-men]. They fled for their lives. When caught, they were shot down in cold blood, or stoned to death, or hung to trees or the lamp posts. Their homes were pillaged; the asylum which Christian charity had provided for their orphaned children was burned....

"How astonishingly has all this been changed. The same men who could not have shown themselves in the most obscure street in the City without peril of instant death...now march in solid platoons, with shouldered muskets, slung knapsacks, and buckled cartridge boxes down through our gayest avenues and our busiest thoroughfares to the pealing strains of martial music and are everywhere saluted with waving handkerchiefs, with descending flowers, and with the acclamations and plaudits of countless beholders....

"It is only by such occasions that we can at all realize the prodigious revolution which the public mind everywhere is experiencing. Such developments are infallible tokens of a new epoch."

[Continued on next page.]

[Continued from previous page.]

Source H

Anti-Lincoln, pro-McClellan campaign poster in the 1864 Election

"Elect Lincoln and the Black Republican ticket. You will bring on Negro equality, more debt, harder times, another draft! Universal anarchy and ultimate ruin! Elect McClellan and the whole Democratic ticket. You will defeat Negro equality, restore prosperity, re-establish the Union! In an honorable, permanent and happy PEACE."

Questions

7. Most of these sources show racism against blacks. List a particular cause for the racism revealed in each source.

SOURCE	CAUSE(S) OF THE RACISM
Source A	
Source B	
Source C	
Source D	
Source E	
Source G (The anti-draft riot part)	
Source H	

[Continued on next page.]

[Continued from previous page.]

8. The Sambo and Zip Coon stereotypes were around before the Civil War. Which of the sources may have been influence by those stereotypes? Explain your answer.

9. Sources F and G show that attitudes seem to have changed about blacks fighting in the Union army. List at least 3 causes for this change in attitude toward blacks fighting.

10. By the end of the war 200,000 blacks had served in the Union Army. In the last months of the war, there were as many black troops in the Union army as there were soldiers in the entire Confederate army. What problems do you think black soldiers faced?

11. Choose any source (A–H) and evaluate its reliability. Remember to use at least 3 criteria for evaluating sources.

Major Sources Used for Lessons

Lesson 1

Cunliffe, Marcus. *The Nation Takes Shape, 1789–1837*. Chicago: The University of Chicago Press, 1959.

Furnas, J. C. *The Americans: A Social History of the United States, 1587–1914*. New York: G. P. Putnam's Sons, 1969.

Lesson 4

van Deusen, Glyndon. *The Jacksonian Era, 1828–1848*. New York: Harper & Row, 1959.

Lesson 6

Blum, John, et al. *The National Experience*, New York: Harcourt, Brace, Jovanovich, 1985, Part I.

"From Farm to Factory," "Farming Was Family Work," and "Making a Living: Factory." Sturbridge, MA: Old Sturbridge Village. (Curriculum Kits composed by the Museum Education Department.)

Prude, Jonathan. *The Coming of the Industrial Order: Town and Factory Life in Rural Massachusetts, 1810–1860*. New York: Cambridge University Press, 1983.

Lesson 7

Godey's Lady's Book, September, 1831. Reprinted in "Primary Sources: Women's History Bibliography" by Charles Moody.

The Lady's Annual Register and Housewife's Almanac for 1841. Boston: William Crosby and Company, 1841. Schlesinger Library, Cambridge, MA: Radcliffe College.

The Ladies' Cabinet of Fashion, June, 1839. Reel 124, Schlesinger Library, Cambridge, MA: Radcliffe College.

Riley, Glenda. *Inventing the American Woman*. Arlington Heights, IL: Harlan Davidson, 1986, Chapter 3 "The Cult of True Womanhood."

Sanders, Beverly. *Women in the Ages of Expansion and Reform, 1820–1860*, from *Women in American History: A Series*. New York: American Federation of Teachers, 1979.

Sanders, Beverly. *Women in the Colonial Era and the Early Republic, 1607–1820*, from *Women in American History: A Series*. New York: American Federation of Teachers, 1979.

Welter, Barbara. "The Cult of True Womanhood: 1820–1860" from *Dimity Convictions: The American Woman in the Nineteenth Century*. Athens, OH: Ohio University Press, 1976.

[Continued on next page.]

[Continued from previous page.]

Lesson 8

"Anti-Suffrage." Vertical File, Schlesinger Library, Cambridge, MA: Radcliffe College.

Evans, Sara M. *Born for Liberty*. New York: Macmillan, 1989. Chapter 5, "A Time of Division, 1845–1865."

Kerber, Linda K. and Jane Sherron DeHart, eds. *Women's America: Refocusing the Past*. 3rd edition. New York: Oxford University Press, 1991.

Riley, Glenda. *Inventing the American Woman: A Perspective on Women's History*. Arlington Heights, IL: Harlan Davidson, 1986. Chapters 4 and 7.

Scott, Anne Firor and Andrew Mackay Scott, eds. *One Half the People: The Fight for Woman Suffrage*. Chicago: University of Illinois Press, 1975.

Lesson 9

Benson, Lee. *The Concept of Jacksonian Democracy: New York as a Test Case*. Princeton, NJ: Princeton University Press, 1961.

Schlesinger, Arthur M., Jr. *The Age of Jackson*. Boston: Little, Brown, 1945.

Lesson 10

Meltzer, Milton, ed. *In Their Own Words: A History of the American Negro*. New York: Thomas Crowell Company, 1964.

Rose, Willie Lee, ed. *A Documentary History of Slavery in North America*. New York: Oxford University Press, 1976.

Stampp, Kenneth, ed. *The Causes of the Civil War*, Revised Edition. Englewood Cliffs, NJ: Prentice Hall, 1974.

Lesson 12

Fogel, Robert William and Stanley Engerman. *Time of the Cross: Evidence and Methods—A Supplement*. Boston: Little, Brown and Company, 1974.

Gutman, Herbert. *The Black Family in Slavery and Freedom, 1750–1925*. New York: Random House, 1976.

Johnson, Michael P. "Work, Culture and the Slave Community: Slave Occupations in the Cotton Belt in 1860," *Labor History*, Vol. XXVII, No. 3, Summer, 1986, pp. 325–55.

Lesson 14

Fitzhugh, George. *Sociology for the South, or the Failure of Free Society*. Richmond: A. Morris, 1854.

[Continued on next page.]

[Continued from previous page.]

Garson, Robert. "Proslavery as Political Theory: The Examples of John C. Calhoun and George Fitzhugh," *The South Atlantic Quarterly*, Vol. 84, No. 2, Spring, 1985, pp. 197–212.

Weld, Theodore. *Slavery As It Is: The Testimony of a Thousand Witnesses*. New York: American Anti-Slavery Society, 1839, pp. 62–63, 77, 125–28. Excerpts reprinted in John Thomas, *Slavery Attacked: The Abolitionist Crusade*. Englewood Cliffs, NJ: Prentice Hall, 1965, pp. 57–62.

Lesson 15

Elkins, Stanley. *Slavery: A Problem in American Institutional and Intellectual Life*. Chicago: University of Chicago Press, 1959.

Fogel, Robert and Stanley Engerman. *Time on the Cross: The Economics of American Negro Slavery*. Boston: Little, Brown, 1974.

Mitchell, Margaret. *Gone with the Wind*. New York: Macmillan, 1937.

Stowe, Harriet Beecher. *Uncle Tom's Cabin*. New York: New American Library, 1981, First published 1852.

Lesson 16

Blassingame, John W. *The Slave Community: Plantation Life in the Antebellum South*. New York: Oxford University Press, 1972.

David, Paul, Herbert Gutman, Richard Sutch, Peter Temin, and Gavin Wright. *Reckoning with Slavery*. New York: Oxford University Press, 1976.

Elkins, Stanley. See citation in Lesson 15.

Fogel, Robert. See citation in Lesson 15.

Winks, Robin, ed. *Slavery: A Comparative Perspective*. New York: New York University Press, 1972.

Lesson 17

Heller, Jonathan, ed. *War and Conflict: Selected Images from the National Archives*, 1765–1970. Washington, DC: National Archives, 1990.

Library of Congress, Prints and Photographs Division, Washington, DC.

National Archives, Washington, DC.

Lesson 18

Fogel, Robert W. and Stanley Engerman. "Further Evidence on the Nutritional Adequacy of the Slave Diet," Unpublished, 1974, mimeographed.

[Continued on next page.]

[Continued from previous page.]

Fogel, Robert. See citation in Lesson 15.

Kiple, Kenneth F. and Virginia H. Kiple. "Slave Child Mortality: Some Nutritional Answers to a Perennial Puzzle," *Journal of Social History*, Vol. X, 1977.

Lieberman, L. S., K. Cargill, and T. Gibbs. "Slave Nutritional Adequacy: An Input-Output Analysis," *American Journal of Physical Anthropology*, Vol. LIL, 1980.

Sutch, Richard. Chapter Six, "The Care and Feeding of Slaves" in Paul David (see citation in Lesson 16).

Lesson 20

Boorstin, Daniel and Brooks Kelley. *A History of the United States*. Lexington, MA: Ginn and Company, 1986.

Jordan, Winthrop, et al. *The United States*. Englewood Cliffs, NJ: Prentice-Hall, 1982.

Lesson 23

Beale, Howard K. "What Historians Have Said about the Causes of the Civil War," *Theory and Practice in Historical Study*, Social Science Research Council Bulletin, No. 54, 1946, pp. 55–102.

Benson, Lee. "Causation and the American Civil War: Two Appraisals," *History and Theory*, Vol. I, No. 2, 1961, pp. 163–85.

Fehrenbacher, Don E. "The New Political History and the Coming of the Civil War," *Pacific Historical Review*, Vol. LIV, No. 2, May, 1985, pp. 117–42.

Gruver, Rebecca Brooks. *An American History*. Reading, MA: Addison-Wesley, 1976, "Interpreting the Causes of the Civil War," pp. 484–87.

Lesson 24

Beard, Charles and Mary R. Beard. *The Rise of American Civilization*. New York: Macmillan, 1927, Vol. II, pp. 3–10, 36–40, 53–54.

Kramer, Kenyon C. *The Causes of War*. Glenview, IL: Scott, Foresman and Company, 1965, "Unit Two: The Civil War," pp. 65–116.

Ramsdell, Charles. "The Natural Limits of Slavery Expansion," *Mississippi Valley Historical Review*, Vol. XVI, 1929, pp. 151–71.

Randall, James G. "A Blundering Generation," *Mississippi Valley Historical Review*, Vol. XXVII, 1940, pp. 3–28.

Rozwenc, Edwin C. *The Causes of the American Civil War*. Lexington, MA: D.C. Heath, 1972.

[Continued on next page.]

[Continued from previous page.]

Stampp, Kenneth, ed. *The Causes of the Civil War*. Englewood Cliffs, NJ: Prentice-Hall, 1974.

Lesson 25

Catton, Bruce. *The Civil War*. New York: American Heritage Press, 1971.

Lesson 26

Beringer, Richard and Herman Lattaway, Archer Jones, and William Still. *Why the South Lost the Civil War*. Athens, GA: The University of Georgia Press, 1986, illustrations following page 274.

"Ethnic Notions of Black Americans," WGBH TV, 1986.

Wheeler, William and Susan D. Becker. *Discovering the American Past: A Look at the Evidence*. Boston: Houghton Mifflin, 1990, Chapter Ten "The Price for Victory: The Decision to Use Black Troops."

